Rescue Me,
He's Wearing a Moose Hat

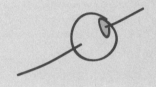

And 40 Other
Dates After 50

Sherry Halperin

SEAL PRESS

Rescue Me, He's Wearing a Moose Hat:
And 40 Other Dates After 50

Published by
Seal Press
An Imprint of Avalon Publishing Group, Incorporated
1400 65th Street, Suite 250
Emeryville, CA 94608

AVALON
publishing group incorporated

ISBN-10: 1-58005-068-9
ISBN-13: 978-1-58006-068-5

9 8 7 6 5 4 3 2 1

Library of Congress Cataloging-in-Publication Data

Halperin, Sherry.

Rescue me, he's wearing a moose hat : and 40 other dates after 50 / by
Sherry Halperin. — 1st ed.

p. cm.

ISBN 1-58005-068-9

1. Halperin, Sherry. 2. Dating (Social customs) 3. Middle aged women—
United States—Biography. I. Title.

HQ801.H315 2005

306.73'0973—dc22

2005014864

Cover and interior design by Domini Dragoone
Printed in the United States of America by Malloy
Distributed by Publishers Group West

To Warren,

I hope you are laughing with the Angels.
You are always in my heart.

Contents

Preface

December 1994
L.A. TIMES
WJF 51 SEEKS INTELLIGENT, HANDSOME, WITTY,
CREATIVE, SELF-ASSURED, FINANCIALLY
SECURE WJM FOR FUN, ROMANCE, AND . . .

I put down the paper. That will never be me. I pity the poor woman who's become so lonely that she has sunk to the depths of personal advertisements. My husband of twenty-six years died a few months ago and my feelings on dating are very simple. I will never do it.

I miss my husband. His death was sudden . . . no time to say goodbye or tell him how much I loved him. I came home from Nordstroms, put down my shopping bags, ate a banana, looked at the mail, went upstairs, and found his still body. In an instant, my life changed.

I went into a necessary robot mode.

Gravesite: Newport Beach with an ocean view. The ocean was important to us. Some of our happiest days were spent on our boat.

Casket: Silver, chosen from a brochure. I couldn't bring myself to go to the mortuary.

Clothes: That was the hardest. My children and I stood in front of his closet, held on to each other, and sobbed. My eldest son, Jonathan, finally chose a navy patterned Hugo Boss tie. It was my husband's favorite. My youngest son, Justin, rummaged through dozens of pants and jackets and finally handed me a navy pin-striped suit, yellow t-shirt, and tennis shoes. I reached into the top draw of the dresser and pulled out a pair of beige bikini undershorts that I had bought for Warren in Paris. The sight of the nude pinup woman on the front changed our tears to smiles.

"Dad would have wanted it this way . . . us laughing and him going out looking utterly ridiculous."

Justin flew to Northern California after the funeral, took one last exam, and drove down immediately to stay with me. He had just finished his bachelor's degree. His beautiful fiancée, Nga, flew from San Jose on weekends to be with us. Jonathan was living in a beach house on Balboa Island with a bunch of young men, all starting their careers after grad school. Outwardly, the boys looked like they were coping, but I knew their world had crashed. They were very close to their dad, a man they loved dearly and looked up to with pride.

There were visits from friends, relatives, neighbors. The refrigerator had enough casseroles to last three months.

Days, then a few weeks went by. I couldn't sleep. I was afraid if I closed my eyes the nightmares would come.

"Do you trust me, Mom?" Justin reminded me of my hippie days in Greenwich Village. It's amazing that tie-dyed shirts and long hair hadn't skipped a generation.

"Of course I do, sweetheart. You're the best."

Candles were lit, lights were turned low. Mellow music played in the background and I shared my first joint with my son. I took a toke and slept for fourteen hours.

> *Note:* Children can become
> the wise parent.

Slowly, I began to reenter the world.

I'm one of the fortunate widows. I was left with some means, which meant I didn't have to sling hash browns or sell shoes. I did, however, have to tighten my belt and think before I spent.

"He's so adorable. What breed?"

"Wheaton Terrier . . . one thousand dollars." The young man at Four Paws handed me the ten pounds of fluff.

I melted. The pup had me at first lick.

"I'll take him." I didn't think. I spent. I guess I had a lot to learn.

Dooley came home with me and became my newest best friend.

I cuddled with Dooley. I took walks with Dooley. I slept on my side of the bed and Dooley slept on my husband's. We ate in front of the television together.

It's when I found myself asking the dog if I should wear the brown or red shirt that I realized how much I missed the companionship of a man.

I also missed the intimacy of sex. But no one could fill the shoes and shorts of my husband. Anyway, who would want me? Nothing on my body is where it used to be. I would need plastic surgery from my kneecaps to my forehead to rectify what gravity and time have done.

I live in Southern California. Need I say more? The priorities in the dating scene here are pretty shallow. Here's what is important to single, eligible men:

- How much money you have
- How much you weigh
- Your bra size
- How fast you put out
- What kind of luxury foreign car you drive
- What kind of SUV your second car is
- And lastly, who you know

At least, that's what I had been told. I hadn't been on a date in twenty-seven years. What did I know? It seemed too hard. It seemed too complicated. No dates. Never!

I vowed to take an oath of chastity. There would be no need for a man in my life. All I needed was to find the single me again and learn to appreciate the person I was before I married. I needed to learn how to feel good about being alone and to get in touch with all those personal inner desires, some of which I was sure were squashed by being part of a couple for so long. I needed to learn that cooking for one was possible. I needed to learn how to balance the checkbook on my new computer, hang a picture, and plunge a toilet.

It would be okay being mono. One would not be the loneliest number. Even though I knew my husband wanted me to have a full life, to date and be happy, I was choosing to be faithful to him for the rest of my life.

Dooley and I would be just fine.

Eight Months Later:

"Hot damn! I have a date!"

I put the phone down and started to plan my wardrobe even though this anticipated date wasn't for more than two weeks.

Peg and Buzz are dear friends. Buzz was my husband's attorney and Peg has been my voice of reason and equalizer for almost twenty years. They both helped me through the grieving process and were always there for me with brilliant advice, lots of hugs, and positive thoughts. How lucky to have good friends.

It was Peg on the phone inviting me up to Palo Alto for a long weekend.

This would be my first "away" adventure. I would drive to the airport alone, fly alone, and visit out-of-town friends alone. I did it all with only one tranquilizer.

So, should I really have called this outing a "date"? The man in the mix didn't actually call to ask me out. It wasn't like, "You fascinate me. Let's have dinner, make passionate love, and get married in three weeks." It had all been arranged.

What makes a date a date?

"Would you mind if Ben joins us for dinner and a movie Thursday night?" Peg asked.

"I'd love it," was my answer.

With cautious excitement and great trepidation, I began to prepare for my first dating encounter in twenty-seven years.

Mr. Moon
"Ben"

I was so nervous. Was my V-necked sweater too low? Oh God, was I really trying to look sexy? My children would die. They picture me as having the scruples of a nun and the looks of a . . . well, a mother.

For the first time in ages, I was aware of my sexuality and it felt damn good. I may have been fifty-one but I certainly did not feel dead.

The doorbell rang. I had remembered Ben correctly. He was tall, dark-haired, and rather handsome. His shoulders looked narrower than I had recollected from our meeting several years before. But that meeting was with my husband and I was seeing him now in a totally different light. When I was married, I looked at men as an entire package. As a single person, I was beginning to notice the parts.

Why are his jacket sleeves so short? My mind had reverted back to ninth grade. I was going to my first high school dance with Norm, the basketball star. It was a Sadie Hawkins, so I had asked him. First school dance or first second-time-around date, it all felt the same . . . scary as hell.

We rode in the backseat, with Buzz driving and Peg chatting up a storm. She was the party planner and I was the guest of honor. I felt compelled to smile constantly, causing my upper lip to stick to my teeth. Did I want Ben to take my hand? Would he want to be alone with me after the movie?

Ben was a perfect gentleman. The movie was about Beethoven's life and he cried openly while we shared a bucket of popcorn and sipped on Diet Cokes. After dinner, we walked and talked and I learned that his true love was his computer and his passion was books. The

"Was my V-necked sweater too low? Oh God, was I really trying to look sexy? My children would die . . ."

chance of this never-married, forty-eight-year-old attorney committing to anything beyond his search to prove that Armstrong never landed on the moon was, well, impossible.

"It was all done with videos. On a movie set," Ben said very seriously, as we strolled a few paces behind Peg and Buzz.

"You honestly believe that? You think the entire world was duped?" I really thought he was joking.

"Of course I do. There is no concrete proof that we landed. All we had were the photos that the astronauts brought back and a couple of rocks. The pictures could have been taken on any set the Hollywood magic makers contrived, and the rocks could have been from your backyard. And the footprints . . . sand doesn't make footprints."

All the while Ben talked, he was staring at the cleavage peeking out from my V-necked sweater.

"Ben, I'm up here . . . and yes, they are real," I said, waving my hand in front of his eyes. "Thank you for a lovely evening."

Painfully shy and truly adorable, my first starting-over pretend date will remain etched in my memory as the only man on Earth to think my 38DDs were breast implants. Peg never intended this to be a fix up. It was all in my mind.

> *Note:* Pretending is good for the
> heart and mind.

Date Two

Turkey Neck
"Morris"

I met Morris at a cousin's wedding in Carmel a few months after the Ben incident. I was seated next to him. His wife was two rows behind. They were separated . . . and not only by the two rows.

As hard as I tried, I couldn't remember anything about meeting Morris, even though we must have talked. That should have triggered a signal that this man was not someone who I would want to socially interact with.

He got my phone number from my cousin and I have to admit I was flattered that he called.

"So, you know I'm separated from Lydia, after almost thirty years. The marriage is damaged beyond repair. No love left. Just fights all the time and . . . "

"I'm sorry. You were married for such a long time," I interrupted. This was getting way too personal.

"Yes, but when it's not right, it's time to move on. And, I would like to move on with you."

I honestly couldn't remember anything about this man. I soon learned that he was a sixty-four-year-old retired engineer. He sounded relatively sane on the phone. He asked me out. I refused. He lived too far away.

He asked me out again and again. I finally accepted. There was this restaurant I wanted to try in Pasadena, about an hour away from my home in Dana Point. Okay, I know it's a selfish reason to go out with someone, but La Bomba was supposed to have great jerk chicken. I just hoped his personality didn't match the featured entrée.

God, I didn't want to be excited, but I was. And again, nervous. This was my first alone date. I shaved my legs, all the way up, and poured myself into tight jeans. I bought a new V-necked sweater that was just low enough. I had lost lots of weight and felt great about my appearance. I was going to nail this guy. I was ready.

At least I thought I was. I had been a widow for almost a year. My body ached for the touch of a man. I wouldn't admit it was my husband's I was longing for. I wanted to be kissed and stroked and hugged. Yes, middle-aged women want all that. Age and widowhood had apparently not wiped out my libido.

I drove to my friend June's home, which was twenty minutes from La Bomba. Before leaving for the restaurant, we made a few strategic plans. June thought she should put on a wig and her bag lady costume (she's not completely nuts, just an actress) and snoop in the restaurant's window to spy.

That mental picture cracked me up and released a lot of tension.

"Stay home. You're insane. Listen, I'll call you at 9:30 PM sharp. If it's a great date, have the Dom ready. If he's a real dud, put the cheap wine on ice."

I pulled up to the restaurant five minutes late and parked at a meter right in front. I panicked; no change in my wallet. I ran into La Bomba praying the meter maid was not hunting on that block. There at the bar sat Morris. Unfortunately, it had to be him. There were no other solo men in the entire place. Trust me, I looked. I

> "Layers and layers of loose skin
> just folded their way from his chin
> to his chest. Was there an Adam's
> apple under it all?"

was so thrown by his appearance that I went out to my car with my acquired change and put it in the slot for the car in back of mine. Out of breath and now totally flustered, I went back into the restaurant and got a few more quarters.

I really don't care what a person looks like. Well, almost. I do care if a man is trying real hard to be someone he isn't. Morris was trying to be John Travolta in *Saturday Night Fever.* His dark blue rayon shirt was buttoned up to his neck. It was three sizes too large. This excess of material allowed me to see the abundance of skin he had around his face. The only way to describe it is Turkey Neck. Layers and layers of loose skin just folded their way from his chin to his chest. Was there an Adam's apple under it all? Did he have to use Q-tips to clean in between the folds? Did the pleats come out in cleaning? It was truly amazing.

I talked and tried to be witty. I stared at his eyes so I didn't have to look at his neck or at the jeans he was wearing, which were way too tight for his skinny legs. He, in turn, kept leaning over, smiling, and tweaking my thigh with his hand. This action should have been reason enough to walk out, but I didn't know how to do that. I was new at this dating game, and after all, he was my cousin's friend.

He thought he was being way cool.

I knew I was in for a double helping of jerk.

Nine thirty. I excused myself and went to the ladies' room, where I called June and told her to open the cheap wine.

I feigned exhaustion, an early business meeting, and dieting as an excuse to skip dessert. We left La Bomba at 9:37 PM.

Then came that awkward moment I imagine many women have experienced.

We're at my car.

He says, "What a wonderful evening."

I smile graciously, my lips sticking again to my teeth.

He leans over to hug me and I think to myself, *Okay, I can handle this. Dinner was good. We can do one of* those man-to-man hugs with a slap on the back.

He comes toward me with his face.

Oh, God, he's going to kiss me. My mind was screaming.

The cheek. I'll give him the cheek. As I veer to the left, he turns my face to the right and plants a juicy, wet, openmouthed kiss on my lips.

It's over. But what the hell just happened?

I got into the car, wiped the spit off my lips, and kept yelling "Oh shit!" over and over as I drove away from my first not set-up date.

At one year, I was nowhere near ready to date. I just wanted to be loved again.

> *Note:* Morris got back with his wife
> and they are living happily in Encino.
> I will never again date a man who is
> separated. The thought of being "the
> other" woman makes my skin crawl.

Date Three

Moose Hat
"Jerry"

Everything about the small beach city of Dana Point reminded me of my wonderful married life. I would pass the cleaners and think of my husband's suits. I would drive by Dim Sum More and fantasize that he was in there getting takeout for dinner. If I was going to succeed at this single thing, it had to be in a completely different environment. I had to create a life for myself where everything was mine and not ours.

I started to read the real estate ads in the Sunday *Los*

Angeles Times. What I needed was a new home and a new beginning.

The page following real estate was the *L.A. Times* Love Connection.

I was fascinated. There was something for everyone. Guys seeking guys! Girls seeking guys! Girls seeking girls! Couples seeking . . . you get the picture? *MEN SEEKING WOMEN*. I combed through the choices and stopped at an ad that read, "I'M READY, ARE YOU?"

I think I'm ready. How do I know? Do I want to date and find a wonderful new man or do I want to replace my husband? Maybe this guy is the one. Since I didn't like the image of becoming the old grandma sitting on the porch in a rocking chair, I had to give it a try.

I dialed the 900 line and nervously left my number.

"It's my first time. I feel like I'm back in high school." I almost gagged as the words came out of my mouth. But I was thinking, *Please look like a cross between Tom Selleck and Peter Jennings and be able to spell "apartheid."*

I used a phony name.

Jerry returned my call the next day and we talked.

> *"And then he appeared . . . wearing a polyester jogging suit and a baseball cap with huge moose ears sticking out from the sides."*

Once, twice, three times. We talked a lot. He seemed to be witty in an East Coast way but always brought the conversation around to sex. He was trying hard to be macho. Or, maybe he was a pervert.

"I've already made love to you," he said the fifth time we spoke. I was fascinated. Part of me wanted to slam the phone down and part of me was titillated.

"Your voice is driving me crazy," he whispered.

If I only had the insight to realize how appropriate the word *crazy* was.

I finally agreed to meet Jerry for coffee at Starbucks. Good old Starbucks. They should open their own dating service. Just think how fun it would be. With every grande latte comes a three-pack of eligible men. Everyone meets at Starbucks.

"Jerry, how will I know what you look like?"

"I'll be wearing a jogging suit, doll, and a baseball

cap." I liked that answer. Casual. Athletic. This might turn out okay.

But "doll"? Did he picture me as the uptight, upright Sarah Brown in *Guys and Dolls*? Or maybe he thinks I'm more like Dolly Levi, the widow matchmaker.

I arrived first and bought my own nonfat, two Equal, grande latte. At a sticky table covered with muffin crumbs, I anxiously awaited my first real blind date. And then he appeared . . . tall, skinny, haggard, and wearing a burnt-orange polyester jogging suit from the eighties and a baseball cap with huge moose ears sticking out from the sides.

"So, you like these designer coffees?" Jerry asked with a decidedly thick New Jersey accent that mysteriously seemed to have escaped me on the telephone.

"Me," he continued before I had a chance to answer, "I like that Asti Spumante stuff. I could drink it all day. Sweet . . . like you, pussycat."

My mother used to call me pussycat. It sounded endearing back then. Now, it sounded dirty. Doll, pussycat? Does this man think I'm a toy or an animal?

"So how's about we catch a flick tomorrow night and then throw down some beers after?" The Moose Hat continued to talk.

"Did I tell you what I do? You'll love this. I have this booth at the swap meet and sell these really cool sun blockers. I swear you would think they were Gucci or that other Italian guy . . . what's his name? Anyways, I get these knockoffs from this guy down in . . ."

I wanted to run. Where was that lovely telephone voice I heard? Who was this weird, unsophisticated, Asti Spumante–drinking man? Where did my Tom Selleck disappear to?

"Jerry, it's been great meeting you, but I've decided to move to Los Angeles and won't be able to date you."

"What, I have some disease?"

"No," I replied. "I'm just allergic to sweet, bubbly wine and moose."

Note: Never jump to conclusions by the sound of a man's voice. I guess I wanted it to work so badly that I only heard what I wanted to hear.

Four months went by. I moved from my quaint beach town to smog-filled, congested, loud, bustling Beverly Hills. The packing was hard. I made four piles of stuff.

1. Take with me
2. Give away
3. Garage sale
4. Hold on to until the last minute and then decide

I felt guilty getting rid of my husband's clothes, tools, and books. I was disseminating bits and pieces of his life and giving it to the Salvation Army. I kept his green bathrobe to snuggle in, along with about fifteen boxes of various things my heart was still attached to.

I loved my new home. It was a New York loft-style condo with walls of glass two stories high. It was chic, cool, in the right location with very friendly neighbors. It felt right. From the minute I opened the front door, I knew it was perfect.

A friend offered me a job working on a television pilot for Fox. It was a pity hire, but that was okay. I welcomed the chance to work again and meet new people. Sadly, the entire crew was under thirty, leaving me only to socialize with my friend, the gay producer.

I wanted to meet men. I felt ready to meet men. So, I did what I swore I would never do. I took out a, oh my

God I can hardly say it, *personal ad* in the *Jewish Journal,* a free newspaper that had a reputation of printing tasteful want ads for love.

I needed to jump-start my new life in a new city.

The paper came out on a Thursday. Ironically, I flew to Northern California that same day to visit my son, who was now married, and his wife. Was I running away?

Curiosity crept in by the time I reached their home. Had anyone answered my ad?

How could I explain to my kids that I was making phone calls to a 900 mailbox number to see if anyone wanted to date their mother?

Answer: I never told them and used my cell phone to make the calls. They shared little about their dating lives. Why should I share mine? Anyway, they probably wouldn't want to know.

By Friday night, there were four calls on the special answering service that the paper had provided. By Saturday night, there were nine. By the time I returned home on Sunday, there were fourteen calls. I had hit the mother lode!

My ad worked, even though I'd stolen the first part

from Moose Hat. *I'm ready, are you? Beverly Hills widowed woman, high energy, fiftyish, creative, attractive, financially secure wanting to meet honest man who loves life and all it has to offer.*

The process of deciphering whether a man could possibly be a date or not a date is quite maddening. The eyes are supposed to be the windows to the soul. So what is the voice? I had been teased before. Does a soft, sexy voice mean that he's a player? How about a deep voice? Does that mean he's all man? What about a timid voice? And who is behind a squeaky voice? What I soon learned was that all the voices were of men who were as lonely and nervous as I was about dating. I answered all fourteen calls.

"Yes, I have been single for a year-and-a-half. Are you single?" When one answered, "No, I'm separated," I quickly explained that I would not date a man who was not legally divorced no matter how long the separation had been. Until a divorce is finalized, there is always an outside chance that the couple could get back together. Another marriage saved. And fairytales can come true. Remember Turkey Neck Morris?

I met with the following three men.

Date Four

Sing-Along with Babs
"Bruce"

Bruce said in his newspaper profile that he was an attorney who didn't practice but taught law. He lived about an hour away from my new condo, so we chose a place halfway in between to meet. I walked into the coffee shop at the Sportsman Lodge and was greeted by a lovely-looking man with a charming smile. We talked for more than an hour about our jobs, our hobbies, and our children. He asked me lots of questions about my show business career and I gladly explained that I had done everything from write television shows to agent aspiring actors. That's what I was currently doing.

"Tell me what stars you've met," Bruce prodded. "Have you been to the award shows?" He continued to delve. "Please tell me you haven't met Liza or Streisand. I'll just die if you have."

"Actually, Bruce, I have met Streisand. It was many years ago. She was sixteen and I was fifteen and doing summer stock at a theater in Fishkill, New York. We both learned to drive on the same old stick shift prop truck. Funniest thing was that my dad used to come up to the theater on Sunday mornings and bring us bagels, lox, and cream cheese. He would always tell Barbra that she wouldn't get anywhere if she didn't do something about her nose."

As I was telling the story to Bruce, I wondered if he was gay.

My date was impressed and asked me out for the following Friday night.

As we walked to our cars, we discussed if we should see a movie, go out to dinner, or both. Then, Bruce suddenly changed the subject.

"You know, I have this tape in the car that I would love you to hear. Do you mind?" His voice was squealing with enthusiasm.

> *"How surreal. I was sitting in a car with a lawyer who was serenading me along with my old pal Barbra."*

What a strange request, I thought. He continued.

"It will only take a minute. Honest. It would mean so much to me."

I was skeptical about getting into a near-stranger's car, but my interest was piqued. I sat in the front seat of his Camaro but kept the passenger door wide open as Bruce sat behind the wheel, started the engine, and turned the tape player on. Suddenly, he burst into song.

"People, people who need people, are the . . . " How surreal. I was sitting in a car with a lawyer who was serenading me along with my old pal Barbra.

He's mad, I thought. Jumping out of the seat, I told him he had a lovely voice and laughed hysterically all the way to my car. I never heard from Bruce again. The Friday date never happened. Maybe he's been discovered and is on the Ozzfest Tour.

Next!

Note: Don't talk about what you do
for a living on a first date if you're a
doctor or in show business.

Date Five

Heat-Packing Doc
"Albert"

A dentist. Look, Ma, I have a date with a doctor.

Albert, number two *Jewish Journal* date, showed up at Starbucks right on schedule. He was short and bald. Our chat over coffee went well enough that we decided to continue at a nearby sushi bar. Now, please note that I hate sushi. I rank eating raw fish on the same level as downing Pepto-Bismol or undercooked liver. But, on first dates, I figure I have to suck it up and do things just to please the man. I don't want to be labeled a JAP.

Overall, the evening was pleasant. No sparks but no bombs.

"Yes, I would love to go out with you again."

A week went by and no call. Then finally, the phone rang and it was Albert.

"How about dinner at Chez Antoine?"

"I would love that, Albert. I've wanted to eat there since I moved to Los Angeles."

"Hope you don't mind if I pick you up in my truck," the dentist asked.

"I love trucks," I lied to him one more time. Trucks have hard seats.

"But," he continued, "I'm just warning you that mine has racks for my guns and I will have the car loaded with camping gear. Right after our date, I'm heading out for a weekend hunt with some buddies."

"Guns? Hunt?" I laughed nervously. I wasn't sure if he was kidding or not, so to be safe, I said I would meet him at the restaurant. Dinner was lovely. The French do know how to present fine food. While enjoying my chocolate mousse, I got the courage to ask about the gun issue.

"It's for real," he answered. "I hunt at least two weekends a month and always have my guns handy. I'm probably the only Jewish hunter in America.

There's something about the chase that's exhilarating. We use the meat for food. You know, donate it or freeze it or . . . "

Albert kept talking and I got sick to my stomach. All the years my late husband and I had a boat, I wouldn't even allow throw-back fishing. If a mouse found its way into our home, we caught it with a live trap and released it in the park . . . along with a cookie for nourishment. *There I go, making comparisons. Not fair.*

I still didn't totally believe Albert until the valet brought up his car. Sure enough, there were rifle racks lining two sides of his enclosed Dodge Ram truck.

Anyone who could kill an animal for sport is not for me. I said goodbye, thanked him for a delicious dinner, and wished him well with his search.

I drove away wanting to send out a red-flag alert to all Bambis and Donalds in California.

> *Note:* When a man says he has a gun,
> and if he doesn't ask you to reach into
> his pocket to check it, believe him.

50 or 60 or 70
"Peter"

I usually believe what someone tells me unless it is so wild that it couldn't possibly be true. I'm trusting.

When a man tells me his age, I accept it as fact, trusting person that I am. After all, I haven't lied about my age . . . yet.

Fifty-one-year-old Peter and I were going to meet at the coffee shop in the Westwood Barnes & Noble. This was a first for me. I was doing Starbucks at an upscale bookstore.

I arrived first. I guess my heart was so into these

"Peter, my third and last newspaper-response date, came in carrying two daisies wrapped in tinfoil. So sweet."

meets and greets that I usually arrived before my date. Or, maybe it was just that my dates were rude or didn't have my amazingly lucky parking karma.

Peter, my third and last newspaper-response date, came in carrying two daisies wrapped in tinfoil. So sweet.

He wasn't fifty-one, or even sixty-one. He was at least seventy-one.

"You're not fifty-one, Peter. Why didn't you tell me the truth about your age?" I really wanted to know.

"Would you have gone out with a seventy-two-year-old man who lives on Social Security?"

That really got me thinking.

What was I looking for? Did he *have* to have money? Did he *have* to be my age or younger? Did he *have* to be skinny or fat or muscular? I had not made out my perfect man list.

I had coffee with Peter, listened attentively to his stories of what L.A. was like fifty years ago, and promised to call him if I had any insurance needs since he was still selling life, home, and health.

As I walked to my car, foil-wrapped daisies in hand, I wondered if I would be as lonely as Peter when I reached seventy-two. Time will tell.

I went home and thought about what I was looking for in a man.

MY PERSONAL PERFECT MAN LIST

1. Taller than five feet, eight inches. I'm five feet, four inches and like wearing small heels.

2. No skinnies. I prefer a man who has some meat on him. I'm quite zaftig and a larger man makes me feel smaller. Okay, I know that's a huge dose of denial but it works.

3. Enough money so I don't have to feel guilty when he treats me to dinner and a movie. It would also be nice if he could pay his own way on a vacation. I do not want to support a freeloader, no matter how delicious he is.

4. Funny—I need a man I can laugh with.

5. Honest—about age, marital status, toupees, illnesses, children, jail sentences, sexual diseases, and sexual oddities. These do not have to be discussed on the first date.

6. If he needs Viagra—fine. Just don't complain about the cost.

7. Loves, not likes, animals.

8. Likes being near the water—loves boats.

9. Has a commonality of beliefs and cultural background with me.

10. Has a good image of himself, is creative, loves his family, and has a life of his own.

I guess I was one of the fortunate ones. I had it all once and wanted it again.

When I started this round of dating, I promised myself I wouldn't compare new men with my late husband. But I was finding that promise impossible to keep.

During my marriage, I became one with the man who fathered my two sons. We thought alike and finished each other's sentences. If we weren't talking about the kids, we were sharing stories about our day.

I probably have two thousand pictures of my late husband and myself. You won't find one where we were not hugging or touching.

Hand in hand, arm in arm. What will the next two thousand pictures of me look like?

Stud Muffin One
"Mike"

Time passed. My dating fiascoes from the personal ad disappointed me so much that I decided to concentrate on work and not love. I was still at the talent agency booking everything from McDonald's to feminine hygiene commercials. At night, I took music classes at UCLA.

It's funny how things happen when you least expect it. One Sunday afternoon, I found myself standing in line at a Starbucks on Pico.

That certainly wasn't unusual, except this time I was not waiting for a date. I turned around to see how long the line had become and locked eyes with a very tall, hunky man right behind me. Some stupid comment came blithering out of my mouth, like "Geez, are they giving away the coffee today?" There had to be fifteen people waiting for their caffeine fix.

In spite of my awkwardness, the man asked if I would like to share a table since it was so crowded. Polite introductions aside and after a few moments of mindless talk, we got down to particulars.

Stud Mike: "I'm a divorced dad of an eleven-year-old boy. Been single for five years. I'm a photographer. You know, weddings, bar mitzvahs, fiftieth wedding anniversaries."

Bells and whistles went off. I was attracted to him. He was wearing Bermuda shorts, a denim long-sleeve work shirt with the sleeves rolled up a bit, and he had the greatest legs, with just enough hair to make them look tan. I knew he was a lot younger than me and wondered why he was flirting.

We talked, laughed, and sipped coffee for about an hour.

Stud Mike fumbled his words.

"Okay, this is that moment when I ask for your phone number and prepare to be knocked down." We

*"I was burning hot,
and this time it wasn't
a hot flash."*

were standing next to my car and he was looking down at his shoes like an embarrassed boy. But before he could finish the sentence, I had a pen and paper out jotting down my seven digits.

He smiled. I smiled.

What a wonderful feeling it was to meet someone I actually liked and was attracted to.

To my delight, Mike called a few days later.

"I'm not much of a cook, but I'd love for you to come over for dinner. How's Saturday night?"

I accepted. "I'll bring some wine."

I had an immediate chemistry with this man. But instead of my enjoying the moment and relishing in the fact that a very handsome, younger man had just asked me out, I spent days wondering why.

Impulsively, I made several dry runs to his address. I hoped to catch a glimpse of him. Was I stalking?

Saturday finally came.

Inside his condo, I found a Hugh Hefner-wannabe love nest. A sheepskin rug lay in front of the old, dark brown velvet sofas. There was a velvet painting above the fireplace, lit candles all over, and vanilla incense burning. Amazingly, I wasn't put off by this. I think I was ready for an evening of high school romance circa 1961.

After a dinner of spaghetti, salad, and wine, we sat in the living room and listened to the sexy voice of Barry White. Stud Mike softly kissed my hand. He kissed my neck and then my lips. It was wonderful. The room smelled of musk and vanilla and for the first time in sixteen months, I felt like a woman. I was burning hot, and this time it wasn't from a hot flash. We kissed deeply and our hands started to explore.

We didn't have sex, but we had some great fun. I needed to be touched and held. It had been so long.

A relationship began. I was the one self-conscience about the age difference. Every time I brought it up, he gently covered my mouth and would say, "Honey, it's only a number." But the number was twelve years.

We had almost nothing in common. I've always considered myself rather worldly; he had been to Mexico once. I loved classical music; he dug alternative. I loved two-week cruises; he could afford to rent a rowboat for two hours. But the sizzle was there and that's what I needed.

I dated Stud Mike on and off for three months and never made love to him. He was frustrated and constantly questioned why I wanted to remain celibate. I explained that I was not ready for that kind of physical intimacy. In my heart, I still felt like I would have been cheating on my husband.

Stud Mike eventually stopped calling me. I was both sad and relieved.

I think women who are widowed in some ways have a more difficult time dating than those who are divorced. Of course, this is the only vantage point from which I can judge. I did not ask to be single. It was thrust upon me. I had no arguments with my husband. I didn't take half his house or half his golf membership or half his children.

The only thing I was angry about was his dying.

I would like to find a new companion. So, I have to date.

But how?

I quit the talent agency. The industry had changed since I had been an agent years before. Now, everything was done with computers and the telephone instead of trips to the studios to meet the casting directors. This was not what I had signed up for and I was not happy.

I was almost a grandma figure in most of the extension classes I was taking at UCLA. How many fifty-two-year-old women compose on electronic instruments? The class was me and twelve twenty-three-year-olds.

I temple-hopped several Friday nights a month. Instead of being religiously inspired, I felt empty and sad. I was mad at God and mad at all the happy parishioners holding their dear ones close. Finally, I was mad at my husband for dying, a very important step on the grief recovery ladder. I would sit in the back of the sanctuary wanting to yell out "Why, God? He was a good man."

Memories would come flooding in and bring me back to the days when Warren and I called our sons "cookie Jews" because we were sure the only reason they were so anxious to go to services was for the cookies afterwards. I didn't care about the reason, I was with my family.

I seldom made it through an entire service and usually walked out in tears. I missed my past life.

To me, it seemed like the whole world was coupled.

More months went by. I took my first solo cruise and found it easy to meet people in that enclosed environment. Even eating alone didn't bother me. This was an accomplishment. I was growing.

But when I returned to Los Angeles, the same problems existed. What can I do with my time and how do I meet a special man? Problem one was soon resolved. My good friend Nanci called and asked me to work for her film company. They took feature films that the major studios were releasing, had them captioned, and distributed them all over the country, so that deaf and hard of hearing people could have the big screen experience and not have to wait until the film came out on video. The job was both challenging and rewarding.

I worked from home, most often in my pj's. Obviously, this job would not lead to meeting an eligible bachelor.

"Don't be single. There are wonderful men in Los Angeles looking to meet you. We specialize in upscale matchmaking for the upscale woman."

I put the newspaper down and immediately made an appointment with the Beverly Hills matchmaking company.

The interview was two hours long. They quizzed me about my life, what I was looking for, and why my dating so far had not been successful.

My mind went back to *My Personal Perfect Man List* and I confided that no one had even come close to meeting my standards. It seemed as though almost every man I had gone out with met part of the list, but I wanted the whole enchilada. I needed help.

The woman told me about their many successes and about the exceptional men ready to meet me. On the walls, there were portraits of happy couples, all supposedly matched by this company. The fee was five thousand dollars for three dates. I wouldn't see pictures of the men but had the option of not accepting a date after we spoke on the phone. When I recovered my composure and realized that it wasn't the Tic Tac in my mouth that I was choking on, I decided that I had no choice but to sign on. The promise of love was just a signature away.

"That's what credit cards were created for," I told the matchmaker.

These men would be screened and selected especially for me. I was sure I would find not only a date but a new husband.

R.O.M. (Rich Old Man)
"Lenny"

A few days later, I was back in the Beverly Hills office of The Matchmaking Mavens.

"Len is a fifty-nine-year-old divorcé living in Brentwood. He says that his home is secluded, behind gates. He owns a flat in London and a beach house in Cabo. I see here that he has a cook, a houseman, and a chauffeur. He is semi-retired, loves the opera and theatre, and has a box at the Hollywood Bowl. He's six foot one and a little overweight, but has a private trainer."

Sophie looked up from the profile she was carefully reading.

"Do you want us to fix you up with him?"

I sat across from the matchmaking lady and thought I was hearing words directly from God. What woman would not want to date this man?

"He sounds too good to be true," I answered.

A few days later, Len called from London.

"I don't have much time to talk now, but let's set a date to meet when I get back to the States. How's Saturday the ninth?"

My heart pounded with excitement.

"I'll have my secretary make dinner reservations at The Regent Beverly Wilshire."

Len's overseas call ended and all I could think about was that he was taking me to the same place where Julia Roberts was romanced by Richard Gere.

Would I be finding my Prince Charming, too?

When the ninth finally arrived, I was a basket case.

This could be it, I thought. The security bell rang in my condo and I looked through my little television screen at the man standing there, waiting to be let in. It was grainy and blurred but I could tell he was tall. I only saw his chin in the monitor. I pushed the buzzer and anxiously awaited for him to arrive at my door.

Since my husband died, I have joked often that I just want a man delivered to my doorstep with a bow around his neck. I would take it from there, training him to be the perfect mate. Maybe this would be the gift I was waiting for?

Riding to the restaurant, I sat and studied Len. He was not fifty-nine years old. More like sixty-five. I've always been very good at estimating age. Why do people lie? Actually, the car smelled of old man. What was that smell? I still have never been able to zero in on it. But I smiled and laughed and kept an open mind.

Over dinner, we told our stories.

I asked him where he was born.

"Philadelphia," he answered.

"How many children do you have?" The answer was three.

"How many times were you married?" Again, the answer was three.

He saw that I was a bit surprised and quickly chimed in, "That's three counting you."

Now that kind of tantalizing answer sparked my interest and piqued my curiosity about Len. This man was clever and cagey.

We started to date. Len took me to L.A.'s best restaurants: Morton's, The Palm, Valentino. We went to movies, the theater, and the opera. But Len had rules.

"Do not expect me to call you every day. When the cook makes us dinner, tell him how much you enjoyed the meal. I have such a terrible time keeping good help."

That should have been a clue.

"Meet me in your parking lot after I buzz you. The hallway to your place is too long for me to walk. Never say anything personal to me in front of the chauffeur."

Len was odd but very intelligent. He could talk about many things. Sadly, the topic he liked most was his two ex-wives.

He was still depressed over the last breakup and really was not ready to start a new relationship. I heard all about his divorce ad nauseam—how much the lawyers cost, how she was sleeping around, how much she finally got from him.

Len was on so many antianxiety and antidepression drugs that I didn't know who he really was. His speech slurred often and he went to sleep at 8 PM.

I finally said, "That's enough. When you are ready to move on and can spend fifteen minutes without ex-wife bashing, give me a call."

Note: When a man bitches, complains, or whines about his ex, he most likely has not dumped his baggage. Look for someone who is traveling light.

One Matchmaking date down; $1,666.66 spent. Two more men to meet.

Date Nine

Stud Muffin One... Again
"Mike"

After dating a man who was twelve years older than me, I was ready to try young again. As I said before, I was very attracted to Stud Muffin Mike and felt bad about the way our dating ended. I remedied that by calling and inviting him to my place for dinner.

"I've never cooked for you, Mike. Come on over and I'll whip up something special. I've missed you."

Candles lit the table; the lights were dim and romantic music played in the background. I did not have dinner in mind. Stud Mike showed up with a headache. I used this to my advantage and offered him a massage. I rubbed, we kissed, and dinner got cold. By the end of the night, I was no longer a widow virgin.

Stud Mike was the best thing that could have happened to me. He made me feel like I was alive and wanted. We had fun. We laughed. The sex was amazing. He could hardly make it through my front door without my wanting to rip off his clothes. I even showed up once at his condo with just a raincoat on. We drove up the coast and made love between two blankets on the beach. This type of whirlwind romance went on for months.

But eventually, I realized that I wanted more. I wanted flowers. I wanted some kind of a commitment. I wanted someone who could say those beautiful three words to me . . . let's go cruising. Mike and I were living in two different worlds and this time, I broke it off. I would miss the play sessions but I knew there had to be someone else out there for me.

Thank you, Stud Muffin Mike.

Note: There's a time to play and a time to realize that recess is over.

The Doctor Is In
"Guy"

Guy was my second set up from the matchmaking company.

"I have a surgeon I'd like you to meet. Interested?" The words came out of the matchmaking lady like a choir of cherubs singing the Hallelujah Chorus.

Note to self: Stop equating great-sounding dates to religious experiences.

But another doctor date did sound perfect. A man who could buy me flowers and afford dinner for two.

"Of course I'd like to meet him. Tell me more."

"Guy was arrogant and had

a huge Napoleon complex . . .

all five feet, six inches of him."

"Well, he's been divorced about three years. He has two teenage children and lives in Pasadena."

Within a day, Guy called. We talked for about ten minutes and he asked if I was free on Sunday for brunch.

"Make a reservation any place you like," he said.

I thought that was a bit strange but figured he was busy taking out gallbladders and kidney stones. I called The Ivy, one of my favorite restaurants in Beverly Hills, and reserved a table on the terrace. Guy picked me up right on time and, after the usual pleasantries, escorted me to the guest parking area of my garage.

"Which one do you think is mine?" he inquired, pointing to the five cars lined up against the wall.

"I have no idea," I answered. "I've only known you five minutes."

"Come on, guess," he prodded.

"I really don't know." I saw he was getting annoyed. "Okay, the silver Mercedes."

"No, it's the rad blue Corvette. My kids think I look ridiculous driving it. What the hell do they know?"

Well, in this case, quite a lot.

Guy was arrogant and had a huge Napoleon complex . . . all five feet, six inches of him. On top of that, he bragged that he didn't pay the dating service a dime and intimated that the matchmaking gals even paid for brunch. What did he have to lose? It was a free date and a free brunch.

At first, I was disappointed. Then, I became furious. How dare they? They were using this single doctor as a shill; someone to tempt their clients and add prestige to their database.

When I challenged the dating service, they admitted that it is routine within the industry to comp certain very eligible bachelors. I felt like saying, *I'm a very eligible woman and you certainly didn't comp me.* But they still owed me one more date and I wanted them to deliver.

Later, when I thought back to my phone conversation with Guy, I wasn't surprised that our date was a washout. There were telltale signs that we would not be a match. He complained about his kids. My first instinct was that he was a jerk. I sensed anger in his voice. He sounded like this entire process was more of a chore than an exciting, potential match. I should have turned the date down. Guess I was too desperate. I was impressed with the package and didn't listen carefully enough to what was inside.

Note: Listen to your first instincts.
They are usually right.

Day after day I walked by my refrigerator and checked *My Personal Perfect Man List*. It definitely needed some revision. Was I being too picky? I had been making some very bad choices. Los Angeles proved to be an aquarium of eligible men. I kept telling myself that it's just about hooking the right fish.

But I was getting tired of throwing in the line.

1. Taller than five feet, eight inches. I'm five feet, four inches and like wearing small heels.

Height is not that important to me anymore. I never wear heels.

2. No skinnies. I prefer a man who has some meat on him. I'm quite zaftig and a larger man makes me feel smaller. Okay, I know that's a huge dose of denial but it works.

What does it matter if a man is skinny or fat? Note to self: Consider a breast reduction. That will help with the zaftig thing.

3. Enough money so I don't have to feel guilty when he treats me to dinner and a movie. It would also be nice if he could pay for his own way on a vacation. I do not want to support a freeloader, no matter how delicious he is.

Does it really matter who pays? I have been thinking like a woman in the Seventies. Mrs. Brady would not have taken a boyfriend on a trip to St. Lucia, but Cher certainly would have a boy toy accompany her on a vacation. If he were her dream man, she would relish treating him to massages, new clothes, and first-class airplane seats. I want to be Cher.

4. Funny—I need a man that I can laugh with.
Still a must.

5. Honest—about age, marital status, toupees, ill-nesses, children, jail sentences, sexual diseases, and sexual oddities. These do not have to be discussed on the first date.

You know, if he has a toupee or a pacemaker, I can live with that!

6. If he needs Viagra—fine. Just don't complain about the cost.

I'll chip in.

7. Loves, not likes, animals.

That tells so much about a man. I'll accept a dislike for cats, but he still has to adore dogs. Maybe it's a licking thing?

8. Likes being near the water—loves boats.

He doesn't have to love boats as long as he accepts my time as Skipper. Maybe he can be my little buddy, Gilligan.

9. Has a commonality of beliefs and cultural background with me.

Still important. Although, a nice Italian or Presbyterian is looking better by the month.

10. Has a good image of himself, is creative, loves his family, and has a life of his own.

This sounds way too Dr. Laura to me. Maybe I should think Dr. Ruth?

Man in Black
"Dan"

Dan contacted me from Matchmaker.com, an online dating service. I had put my profile on the site thinking I needed a new avenue of exposure. He didn't post a picture but sounded very nice when we finally talked on the phone. We had something in common in that we both were in the entertainment industry. Dan produced local news programs. I was still distributing feature films.

The Soup Plantation was his suggestion for dinner. I couldn't believe how good-looking he was as he walked toward the table where was already seated. The fact that he was on the short side didn't bother me. I was adhering to my new *Personal Perfect Man List.*

What did seem a bit strange was that everything he wore was black—sunglasses, shoes, socks, pants, shirt, jacket, and hat. At first, I thought he may be a Hasidic Jew but soon realized it was just his Hollywood statement. After we got past the show business connection, there was nothing to talk about. I knew I wasn't hip or pretty enough to date this man. At least, that's how he made me feel.

Dinner was tense. I was happy when the bill came and it was over.

I never heard from Dan again. Nothing funny happened. Nothing terrible happened.

That was the problem . . . nothing happened.

> *Note:* Just because you are in the
> same profession doesn't necessarily
> mean you have something in common.

By now, I had discovered lots of sites for computer dating. There was Jdate (Jewish Dating), Match.com, Matchmaker.com, MillionaireMatch.com, e-harmony.com, etc. For me, and for many women I have talked to who are dating in the second half of their lives, this forum provides a safe, interesting, and palatable way to meet men.

Does it work? I know several women who have met and married men from online services.

The mother in me insists I give you some little safety tips if you decide to jump into this particular dating pool. When you find someone who you think is yummy, don't rush into a one-on-one meeting. Send emails and find out tidbits about his background. Never tell him anything in these notes that would enable him to locate you. Actually, I have always used my middle name as an introduction and have never said where I live or what my phone number is.

Next, you want to talk on the phone. It's usually the man who is willing to give you his number, so try to get it before he asks for yours. It's only after several phone conversations and a feeling of interest and comfort that you should agree to meet. And, this should happen always in a very public place and usually miles from your home. When you leave the date, make sure you aren't being followed.

It's just plain safe and sane. Mother has spoken.

Jumpsuit
"Jim"

Jim was on Jdate.com. He was retired and looked rather distinguished in his serious online picture. We agreed to meet at a coffee shop in a West L.A. shopping center at 7 PM.

I waited anxiously, like I did most dates. I still believed that Mr. Right Again was out there, and every date meant the possibility of meeting the man I would grow old with.

I was seated at a table and already had bought my own coffee when Jim walked over and introduced himself.

Oh, poor Jim. God had not blessed him with taste in clothing nor teeth to admire. He wore a jumpsuit. Yes, the kind a mechanic or a man in a 1970s time warp would wear. It was navy blue, belted at the waist, and unzipped halfway down his chest. When he smiled, a canyon appeared between his front teeth.

I smiled back, he sat down, and we started to talk. I brought up the fact that I love to travel. He brought up the fact that he had false travel agent documents that he used for getting cheap hotel rooms. He also passed himself off as a decorator, a plant doctor, and several other things using phony business cards to get discounts. Why pay retail when a little piece of paper can get it for you wholesale?

At that point, I got up, thanked him for meeting me, and left. The entire date was eleven minutes.

> *Note:* A bad date can never be too
> short. Time is precious.

Would You Believe?
"David"

One late evening when sleep wouldn't come, I cranked up the computer to distract my hyperactive, overly creative mind. Seventeen solitaire games later, I decided to do a bit of surfing and found AOL Love Connections. For some unknown reason, I started to check out personals in Northern California and stumbled on an intriguing ad:

"Successful male, 55 yrs old, looking for interesting, vivacious, educated, worldly woman. I am on the

board of my Yacht Club, have season tickets to the
San Francisco Opera, and ride a Harley.
Email me back. You won't be sorry.

I emailed him immediately and asked if some lucky woman had already snapped him up or was he still in the dating market.

By morning, David had written back and we started to correspond several times a day. I would check my computer every two hours to see if I had a letter. He sounded so perfect. I was fascinated with this man. My heart was again racing. He said he lived near San Francisco, was in the tech business, was semi-retired, and had lots of free time to travel and enjoy life.

After nine emails and three days, he asked for my telephone number. I wrote back that he should send me his, preferably at his office. I could then find out if he was really employed.

An email popped up within minutes with a work number and message telling me that I should use Jones as my last name. As usual, I had given David a phony first name and no last.

I called and a secretary answered.

"This is Lee Jones calling David . . . " I didn't know his last name.

A man's voice answered and the chatter began.

We were both originally from New York.

We both loved boats. He had a fifty-eight-foot Bertram. I used to have a fifty-three-foot Hatteras.

He had a grown son and I had two.

He told me that his name was David Rosenblum and then asked what my last name was.

I told him.

There was silence.

"Interesting. I have relatives in New York by that name," he offered.

"I do too," I chimed in.

"You don't by any chance know a Jerry or Warren Halperin, do you?"

I could hardly catch my breath. I was shaking.

"I was married to Warren," I answered slowly.

"Lee, or whatever your name is, I think we're cousins by marriage."

I had found my late husband's long-lost cousin David and was flirting with him. Was this kismet? Had my husband ordained that I find this man to keep me in the family?

I suddenly remembered meeting David many years earlier when he, his then wife, and his young son visited our home in Newport Beach. Actually, what I remembered most was his son carrying a small golf club and using the flowers in the backyard as practice balls.

David had developed some kind of computer gadget in the early 1980s and was said to be very wealthy and rather eccentric.

When we both recovered from the news of this amazing connection, David invited me to fly up to San Francisco the next day.

"Where should I make hotel reservations?" I asked.

"Don't worry, I have a 10,000-square-foot house. You'll stay with me."

"I can't stay with you, David."

"I have a full-time staff. You will be perfectly safe. Listen, I have an early-morning meeting in Seattle, so I'll have my secretary arrange a flight to get you to San Francisco around noon. I'll be arriving back at SFO around 11:50 AM."

"How will I know you?" I questioned.

"I have red curly hair, will probably have on a long

black coat, and will be carrying a brown briefcase. Ciao, baby. It's going to be fun."

I was giddy with excitement.

The next day, I stepped off the plane and, optimist that I am, started to search for my next love. By the time the entire plane had emptied and there were no more people in the waiting area, my heart sank with expectations of being stood up.

My cell phone rang.

"It's Trudy, Mr. Rosenblum's secretary. He missed his flight from Seattle and suggested you get some lunch. He'll meet you in front of T.G.I. Friday's at 2:00 PM."

Okay. I could certainly understand this slight delay.

I sauntered over to the airport restaurant, rollaboard suitcase in tow, and had a spinach salad, making sure no green stuff was left between my teeth.

David arrived at 2:10. He was about five feet, five inches, very round, and wore the most outrageous suspenders I have ever seen. They were green and yellow with dollar signs climbing from his belly, over his shoulders, and down his back to his waist. He had thick, very curly red hair that was long, wild, and unruly. As we walked to his huge Bentley, I realized he actually waddled from side to side, which I found quite endearing.

"Since I hadn't brought a bathing suit, and David was standing on the deck completely nude, I just slipped my towel down and went into the Jacuzzi au naturel."

The evening was fascinating. I was taken by David. He had one of the most brilliant minds I have ever encountered and his quirkiness was sexy to me. After Astrid, his Tyrolean-looking Swedish cook, served dinner, we retired to his wing of the house. There, we enjoyed a Jacuzzi and wine on his patio overlooking the Golden Gate Bridge and San Francisco Bay. It was amazing. There were stars overhead and the bay crashing below.

Since I hadn't brought a bathing suit, and David was standing on the deck completely nude, I just slipped my towel down and went into the Jacuzzi au naturel. This normally would have bothered me, but since David was such a roly-poly, I looked liked Twiggy in comparison. We toasted the evening with champagne and kissed in the moonlight.

I retired to my own suite with thoughts of a relationship that looked very promising.

But the next day took a bit of a turn. David had a business meeting, so he passed me over to Astrid, who took me shopping in Tiburon, a quaint artsy town. After walking around for a bit and buying a few things, we stopped for lunch at a local place on the water.

"You know he is very different. He's had many girlfriends and all have left him."

I couldn't believe what David's housekeeper was saying.

She continued, "I've been with him for fifteen years. You'll see. Don't get caught up with his money. He's not a nice person."

I wondered why Astrid was bashing David. Was she in love with him? Was she jealous of all other women who came onto her turf? Or did she really know the true nature of her boss and want to save me time and heartache?

If I told David what his employee said, he wouldn't believe me. After all, he had a working relationship with this woman for many years and I was a brand-new acquaintance. So, I decided to just file away what Astrid said and see where the journey led.

There was a lot of banging going on that night. *Bang!*

Bamp! Thump! David was fascinated with the rhythm of drums. He probably had twenty of them in the living room and we spent at least an hour playing congas, bongos, and *doumbeks.* We danced to Tony Bennett around the indoor pool and drank martinis until we both could hardly make it to bed. No guest quarters for me.

I snuggled next to David under the fluffy, soft down covers. The windows were open and the surf crashed below.

"Does my weight bother you?" he asked.

"No. I'm just concerned about your health." All the while, I was wondering how it would be to make love to him. Would I be crushed under that walrus belly, never to breathe on my own again? How would I ever be able to find his penis?

"I can't do this," David barked.

Was David having an attack of conscience?

"I'm used to sleeping alone."

"I'll stay on my side of the bed," I offered, moving away startled.

"No, it's not that. You see, I have this stomach problem and at night, I . . . " David became embarrassed. I looked at this gazillionaire in amazement that anything would make him self-conscious.

"Okay, I fart. I fart all night. I'm the king of farts. By morning, I'll stink up the entire room. I'm a human exterminator."

I bit my lip so I wouldn't laugh in David's face.

"I get the picture," I offered, as I hurried to the guest bedroom where I immediately opened the window and enjoyed the very fresh night air.

Throughout breakfast, Astrid gave me darting looks. It was evident that I was intruding on her territory but I didn't give a damn. She was the help and I was the invited guest who slept for fifteen minutes with her boss.

After a morning of sightseeing, we headed to the airport. It seemed like we had gone only a few miles on the freeway when David pulled over and stopped at a bus stop.

"The shuttle will pick you up here in fifteen minutes. It will take you directly to SFO."

"You're not driving me?" I asked in disbelief.

"Have a business meeting. It's been fun. I'll call you, Cuz." David leaned over to give me a kiss on the cheek.

I was dumbfounded. This man I had played with all weekend was sending me home on a bus. He could have called a cab or ordered a car. But no, the fat, farting gazillionaire chose public transportation.

I was confused and felt terribly rejected. Would I see this man again? Did I want to? Was I just attracted to his money or did I really enjoy his company? On the bus, I took a hard look at the situation and decided that, quirky behavior and all, he was who he was. Yes, to my astonishment, I wanted to explore David some more.

But I wondered if the bus drop-off was really a brush-off? Maybe David didn't want to explore me.

Note: When fate rears its head,
be ready for the ride.

The Return of R.O.M.
"Lenny"

But David didn't call. I emailed and thanked him for the weekend. There was no answer.

Meanwhile, it had been months since I had heard from Len, the wealthy older man who talked about his exes all the time.

"I have courtside seats for the Lakers game tomorrow night. Nicholson is three seats away. Keaton, four."

"I have plans," I replied, which I did.

"Cancel them. You'll have more fun with me."

I liked a man who took charge and Len, if nothing

else, worked diligently to get what he wanted. "I've changed. . . . Give me another chance. I think about you all the time." His voice seemed sincere.

Len picked me up in his limo and we held hands all the way to the game. Maybe I hadn't given him enough time.

For five months, he wined and dined me.

I wasn't dating anyone else. All of my dot-com dating services were put on hold. When we were at a concert or a film, everything was great. He couldn't talk. But over dinners or on walks, the conversation was always about him, his frustrations, and his ex-wives. Why did I put up with this? Was I so lonely that I accepted his downfalls more than I respected my own feelings? Most often, I was happier leaving dates with Len than I was anticipating them.

Then one evening at Spago, a tony restaurant in Beverly Hills, Len cleared his voice and said, "Marry me. I'll give you one million dollars and an allowance of twenty-five thousand a year for clothes. All I want is for you to be by my side."

I was dumbfounded. A proposal. It wasn't the romantic kind, down on one knee with a diamond being

"I have courtside seats for the Lakers game tomorrow night. Nicholson is three seats away. Keaton, four."

slipped on my left hand. If Len wanted to get down on one knee, he would have had to ask the waiter to help him back up. Someone wanted to marry me again. It took my breath away.

It would have been easy to say yes. I would have been taken care of for the rest of my life. That's what this business deal promised.

But I wasn't in love with Len. I felt more like his shrink than his girlfriend.

"I'm very flattered, Len, but I can't marry you."

"Why? You won't get a better offer. I'm a hell of a catch."

"Len, what's the name of my dog?" I quietly asked.

"Spot?" He chuckled loudly.

"Wrong. I'm being serious. What company do I work for? Where was I born? And what are my children's names? You don't know, do you? And that's because our relationship is all about you. You're a brilliant man who has a huge capacity to love. And someday, you'll meet the right woman and you will remember her dog's name."

We finished our dinner and the chauffeur drove me home.

I kissed Len on the cheek and said goodbye, sure he knew that our relationship was over.

I turned down a wedding. Even though he was the wrong man, it was still nice to be asked.

Note: Don't be blinded by what
you think you want.

The Bagel Man
"Steve"

Over the next few months, I dated three forgettable men. Maybe bad dates come in threes . . . like good fortune and death.

Steven and I met at my favorite frozen yogurt store on the corner of Westwood and Pico. He was short, thin, and bald . . . two strikes according to *My Personal Perfect Man List,* which I had memorized and now chanted as my new mantra.

I stood at the counter really wanting an extra-large chocolate chunk, my favorite flavor. But with a new

> "He was short, thin, and bald . . . two strikes according to My Personal Perfect Man List, which I had memorized and now chanted as my new mantra."

date by my side, I controlled my passion and modified my order.

"I'll have a small chocolate chunk and no toppings."

Steve ordered a banana split with extra whipped cream. I already hated him.

"So, Steve, you own a bagel shop?"

I was sure his answer would be "Yes," since his online handle was Bagelpro.

"Oh no, I really just love bagels. In fact, I'm somewhat of a connoisseur on the subject. I'm an accountant. Tax specialist. Very boring."

On our little walk after finishing the yogurt treat, Steve gave me a lecture on the history and advancement of the bagel. Nice to know, but certainly not what I wanted to hear. Every time I asked a question, the answer was extended by some other fact about the donut made of dough.

"I've been divorced for three years. Did you know that the first recorded information on the bagel stems back to 1610? Amazing. It was in Poland that women learned to . . . "

I zoned out and decided to tally our walk as part of my daily exercise.

When we said our goodbyes, I went back in the yogurt shop for another chocolate chunk. This time, it was large and smothered with hot fudge and almonds.

Note: Be honest. If the real you
wants to supersize, do it from
date number one.

Natty, Naughty
"Bernie"

Three weeks later, I went out with Bernie. I had answered an ad in a local Beverly Hills newspaper, and after chatting several times on the phone, we decided to meet for brunch.

Bernie was an attorney, loved sports, and seemed to be very bright. It was a lovely Sunday morning. We met at a park in Santa Monica and then walked to a restaurant near the ocean.

He was wearing white slacks, a multicolored pastel shirt with the sleeves rolled up several times, and a violet

> "He looked like a man straight out of a GQ ad. You know, the one who looks like he has just showered at the club after winning his tennis match."

sweater thrown over his shoulders, tied in front. He looked like a man straight out of a *GQ* ad. You know, the one who looks like he has just showered at the club after winning his tennis match. He was definitely much better dressed than I was, and prettier, too.

Brunch was spent talking about how hard it was to meet quality people in Los Angeles and how much easier it must be in cities like Tulsa and Kansas City. All surface talk. Bernie didn't seem eager to let down his guard.

In contrast, one of my weakest traits is that I often say too much too soon. I share so many details about my life that it leaves little to be learned on future dates. I must learn to be more secretive, a trait many men seem to find seductive.

"There's a little art house around the corner on Main. How about catching a film?" Bernie seemed genuinely interested in our date continuing and I was thrilled.

"Sure, I don't have anything planned this afternoon." And there I went, saying too much. What would have been more appropriate would have been to call home on my cell and pretend to cancel an afternoon date with a friend. Being too accessible can look too needy.

The film was Swedish with subtitles. What I thought would be a romantic drama, frame by frame turned into a downright soft-core porn flick. I didn't know if I should be turned on or off. *An inappropriate first date,* I thought.

Then, this gorgeous man's hand started to roam. First it was just a hand resting on my leg. I gave it a pat and lifted it away. Then, this wandering appendage sought to find a warmer area between my legs.

"Are you insane?" I said in a very audible voice as I jerked his hand away.

The only other couple in the theater quickly looked in our direction.

"Shhhhhhh. Don't make a scene. I won't do it again. Weren't you getting turned on?" Bernie whispered.

As I got up to leave, I firmly took Bernie's hand and placed it solidly on the bulge between his legs.

"Enjoy yourself."

I walked out of the theater and chuckled at the thought of the pretty boy inside being arrested for masturbating in public.

"But officer, I'm a lawyer. My date set me up. Have mercy!"

The scene played out perfectly in my mind.

Mercy my ass. Here's Pee-wee's phone number.

Note: Perverts come in all shapes, sizes, and colors, handsome and ugly, educated and not. On a first date, keep to an English-speaking film (for which you've read the review).

Oy, the O.B.
"Seymour"

It must have been a week later when Seymour called.

"I'm a friend of Doug, your dentist. You told him it was okay to call."

"Hi. Yes, I did say that. How are you?"

"Fine, for an old man who was up all night delivering twins. Doug told me a lot about you. It would be great to get together."

A few days later, we met in Brentwood for dinner.

"Should I call you Seymour or Sy?" I was praying for the latter since Seymour was just too New York Jewish for me to handle.

"Sy is fine. Tell me about yourself."

What a joy it was that a man was asking about me.

"Well, I've been in California most of my life. Originally from New York. Studied drama at . . . "

Sy's cell phone rang. "Hold that thought." I started my Greek salad as the doctor turned away from the table.

"No, Mrs. Ornstein, you are not in labor. It's probably gas. Call me if the pain doesn't go away in an hour." Sy turned back. "Sorry. She's only four months pregnant. First baby. Now, where were we? Yes, yes, yes, I did my premed at NYU and then went to UCLA for med school. That's how I ended up in California in 1960 . . . "

So much for finding a man who will let a woman lead.

Seymour was charming. He was smart and witty. But when the stories came around to his profession, I drew the line. Part of me really did want to know what was the most unusual thing he had ever found inside a woman's vagina, but modesty prevailed.

There's just something about dating an OB-GYN that made me uncomfortable. I guess it was my intimate knowledge that when he took my hand in his, I could picture where it had been a few hours before.

Sy never called again. Guess I didn't laugh enough at his jokes.

I called Doug the dentist and thanked him for the fix up.

"Check your patient list. If you have any single investment brokers, artists, plumbers, or ENT docs, send them my way."

Doug was done with playing matchmaker.

Note: I have a new appreciation for the phrase, "A bird in the hand is worth two in the bush."

Date Eighteen

Cuz Comes Calling
"David"

The phone rang.

"Do you recognize my voice?"

I knew it was David immediately. His New York accent was very thick.

"Hello, David. It's been a long time."

"I'm having a Labor Day party. Come up and be my date. Please? My brother and his wife will be here from New York. You'll get to meet some more relatives."

I didn't think I should go and yet I wanted to. David had some obvious great qualities. He was smart, rich, alive, and available. On the downside, he was rude and arrogant. The rich and alive won.

I flew up to San Francisco on September 2, ready for a weekend of hot dogs, wine, and fun. As I exited the plane, my cell phone rang. This scenario was getting boring.

"Listen, I'm tied up in a meeting. So, take the 12:45 PM Tiburon shuttle and I'll pick you up. Get off at Monterey. Sorry, hon."

I was livid. I wanted to turn back and get on the next flight home. Instead, I found the shuttle, paid my eighteen dollars, and rationalized again that David was very quirky.

As the bus pulled up to the Monterey exit, I saw my date standing there, wearing paisley shorts that looked more like silk underwear. True, it was warm, but couple that with a tank top on his rolly-poly, hairy, curly-topped body and the vision was more cartoon trash than Golden Gate wealth.

"We need to go grocery shopping. Astrid left this morning for Sweden and I need you to fix some food for

"He was smart, rich, alive,
and available. On the downside,
he was rude and arrogant.
The rich and alive won."

the barbeque. Barbara, my sister-in-law and your cousin by marriage, may help, but don't count on it. She's quite the priss."

That was it. He knew Astrid was leaving before his party. Being too cheap to hire a caterer, he invited me to cook, clean, and hostess.

As I walked the aisles of Albertson's, I decided that I would take the first flight I could book home the next day.

At dinner, I was cool. David wore the same silk shorts to the lovely, upscale restaurant in Marin that he had on when he picked me up. You could cut the tension between us with the steak knife I was using on my prime rib, the most expensive thing I could find on the menu. I needed beef to soothe my anger.

No hot tub that night. It was bed at 9:00 PM, alone in the guest quarters.

Nothing went right on Labor Day. For starters, I jammed the elevator that led from the main house down to the pool area. David was furious. He didn't yell but paced back and forth while trying to figure out how to get it fixed on a national holiday. Luckily, his brother hit the right buttons, pushed the door, and it started up again.

Then David left several bags of groceries in the car from the previous day's grocery haul. He probably hadn't carried bags into the house since high school. There would be no salad since the lettuce was wilted, the avocados had turned brown, and the tomatoes were mush. And, there would be no hamburgers or hot dogs unless David planned to kill his guests with rancid meat.

Meanwhile, I was on the phone with American changing my plane ticket to 3:00 PM.

I packed without David noticing and called a cab.

"I'm leaving, David. Have a nice party."

"You can't go. Who's going to cook? What should I cook? Look at the mess."

"In a word, David . . . Domino's."

I walked to the curb, suitcase in hand, feeling like I was in charge. Barbara, the sister-in-law, followed me out, bolstering my decision.

"You're too good for him, honey. He's a user. He's the bottom of the barrel. He's yesterday's lunch. By the way, here's my card. I'm hoping to go public with a new software product and looking for investors for the IPO. You're worth more than a mil, right?"

"Thanks, Barbara, I'll pass it on to my people."

What people? I just wanted to get out of there. Now I knew why this crazy branch of the family never connected with all of the mildly neurotic relatives I knew.

I hired the cab to drive me all the way to the airport. No shuttle for me. I'm worth more.

I'm worth more. I'm worth more. I kept saying it over and over as the cab drove me to SFO. This time, I believed it.

Note: To be used is to lose
your control. To lose your
control is to surrender.

Lights, Camera, Pot
"Edward"

Edward was a television producer with a show on prime time. He was tall, thin, wore glasses, and had a great smile. We met online and were sure we had to hook up. After all, we had so much in common and knew so many of the same people.

Our first date was dinner at La Scala, a Beverly Hills restaurant that made the greatest chopped salads in the world.

"You've really got a hit on your hands," I said, realizing that men like their egos inflated.

"Yeah, but the star is an ass." I didn't expect that answer.

"You know, it's all about him and how many pages he has, and his makeup, and his designer suits."

"Don't you want him to be concerned with those things?" I asked, playing dumb.

Ed just shook his head like it was all too much for him. I learned that he had been married twice before and that he still was "best friends" with both. He had two children whom he shared very little about. I, meanwhile, rattled on about my kids, their accomplishments and how important they are in my life. But Ed was unable to shake his thoughts about the arrogant star he had to work with. Nothing I said seemed to register with him. So, our date was mostly shop talk. I felt like a sounding board for his work frustrations.

"Have you ever worked with Dick Clark?" I asked.

"He's not real. He's a robot that McDonald Douglas created."

"Stop that. He's not. He was a great boss. I did a show with him for over a year." I defended Dick.

"How about those Daytime Emmys last week. Did you ever think Oprah would take her name out of the running?" I struggled to find conversation.

"Who gives a shit?" The four-letter words kept rolling off Ed's tongue like they were nursery rhymes.

Okay, this is not a nice man.

When the date ended, I never expected to hear from Edward again.

But a few days later, the phone rang and Eddie wanted me to come over for a drink and watch his show. I said yes, thinking our first date may have just been an apparition. I showered, changed, and showed up at his condo an hour later. It was Tuesday, and the credits had just started to roll.

"Yeah, hi. Come on in. Shhhhh. The show just started. Sit."

For the next half hour, I sat on the couch listening to Eddie yell at the screen.

"You bastard. I told you to cut that line. Why didn't the editor catch that? I can't take this. Did you hear how he delivered that joke?" Eddie didn't give me a chance to answer and continued to converse with the television.

"You egotistical jerk. You almost tripped over that fucking chair. Did you see that? You, you . . . I can't take any more of this."

Eddie disappeared into the bathroom. I sat on the couch, knowing my first opinion of him had been correct.

When he finally emerged, he was much more relaxed. There was telltale white powder just inside his nose and he was taking long, deliberate tokes on a thin, handmade joint. Flashback to the 1960s. My eyes couldn't believe what I was seeing. I was shocked, then disappointed.

He acted like I wasn't there. As he poured himself some wine and sat next to me on the couch, I quietly got up and left. He didn't say goodbye. I didn't say goodbye. I just walked out.

I don't know if I was more upset at his actions or disappointed that he didn't offer to at least share the joint. I would have turned it down, but it would have given me a great exit line.

Note: What could a man possibly think is attractive about being drugged out? What is attractive is being real.

Date Twenty

The Shrink
"Bradley"

It was time to cash in the last of my three purchased dates from the Beverly Hills matchmaking ladies. Both the Rich Old Man and the Doctor were in love with themselves and proved the adage that the menu looked better than the main course. This time, I would be the queen of shrewd. I would spend lots of time on the phone grilling the suspect . . . all the while remaining feminine and lady-like, of course.

Ring. I answered.

"Oh, hi, Bradley. Sophie said you would be calling."

"*I had been taken*

in the name of love."

"Hi. So, they think we're a match," he replied good-naturedly.

"Apparently. Do you mind if I ask you some questions?"

"Of course not. Ask away." Bradley was polite.

I took out my three-page list and started to fire away.

"How old are you, Bradley?"

"I'm sixty-four."

Strike one for the matchmakers. "Sophie said you were fifty-nine."

"Sophie is wrong. I was when I first contacted them five years ago."

That's not a huge difference in age. I'll give him a star in the positive column for telling the truth, I thought.

"You have homes in Huntington Beach and Big Bear, right?"

"No, I sold the place at the beach a few years ago

and only live in the mountains now. Wonder why they said that? They obviously haven't updated my profile."

I was also starting to wonder.

"Brad, you are a psychiatrist?"

"No, psychologist. Retired now." He paused. "I feel like I'm on the firing line."

"Just one more question. When was the last time you heard from the matchmaking ladies and how tall are you?"

"That's two questions. About four years ago." He cleared his throat. "And five feet four. I'm coming into town next Thursday. Should we make a date?"

That was it. No doctor, no beach house, no fifty-nine years old, and a shorty.

"I don't think so, Brad. Nothing against you. I've been lied to by Sophie and if I accept a date with you, they win. By the way, did you pay for their service?"

"No."

That was it. I said goodbye to Brad and immediately called Sophie. I had been taken in the name of love. All Sophie cared about was fulfilling her contract by getting me my third date within the one-year time frame.

I was mad and crushed. They didn't have my best

interest at heart. They had no special man for me. I was just another number on their list of fools.

"Sophie, please? This is Sherry calling."

I had now advanced to furious. I wanted to start screaming but knew I would get much further by staying calm.

"Hello, Sophie. We have something serious to discuss. Do you want to do it on the phone or in person?"

"Phone is fine."

Sophie immediately sounded nervous.

I continued. "You know, I have a lot of friends in the media who would love this story. Just imagine the headline—*Matchmaking Business Busted.*"

Twenty minutes and one Xanax later, I had achieved success. They agreed to give me back half of my fees in exchange for not taking it to the press.

I paid $1,250 for each of the two dates they arranged for me. But what I learned was worth a million.

Note: Love can't be bought.

Date Twenty-One

Nudy Patudy
"Morey"

I met Morey at a health food restaurant on Wilshire in Santa Monica. His business was selling adult toys that he manufactured in China. His hobby was going to a nudist colony in Topanga Canyon. I found out this provocative information over an avocado and sprout salad five minutes into our date.

My mind switched immediately into overload, and it became blatantly clear why none of these facts was in his online Love Connection profile. I also knew immediately that Morey was not the man of my dreams. How on earth

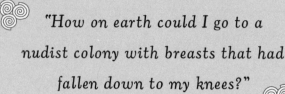

> *"How on earth could I go to a nudist colony with breasts that had fallen down to my knees?"*

would I explain to my family that I was dating a man in the porno business? But more important, how on earth could I go to a nudist colony with breasts that had fallen down to my knees?

Morey asked if his business bothered me. I confessed that it did. As we left the restaurant, he tried to put me at ease by offering me anything I wanted from his high-end line . . . at a sizable discount. Did he have samples of dildos and mink-covered handcuffs in the trunk of his car? I was tempted for a moment but turned the offer down, as well as any future dates.

Note: When you buy porno, it should be with sunglasses and a wig, fifty miles from where you live.

Every day, I stared at *My Personal Perfect Man List* on the refrigerator. Over the months, I had scratched out words and made changes. I was clarifying what was important to me, what I could live with or without. The words became simpler . . . nice, sweet, kind, giving. The list was getting tattered as I was becoming stronger.

I became active in several charities and felt good doing work to help others. I wrote music and recorded a CD in honor of my late husband. There were no grandiose ideas of the CD going commercial. It was done for my children as a tribute to their dad.

I found the companionship of girlfriends soothing.

I stopped looking for a man.

Until . . .

M.O.D.
(Man of Destiny)
"Ben"

Remember Peg, my friend who I thought fixed me up with Mr. Moon Ben, the man who thought I had fake boobs? Well, she called all excited one day telling me about someone she had met in Carmel. He had recently broken up with a friend of hers and she immediately thought of fixing him up with me. God forbid an eligible man be left single for more than a week!

"He's perfect for you. He's retired, Irish, and very good-looking. Can I give him your number?"

I was ready for a good date.

Bill called and we talked.

"Lucky you, living in Malibu," I offered, exuding tons of energy.

"Yeah," was his reply.

"I hear you were in construction."

"Yeah."

"Well, call me some time if you'd like to have coffee." I just wanted to hang up.

"Sure."

There was no connection. He obviously wasn't over the woman he had just broken up with.

It's said that the best way to meet someone is through people who know you well. Peg certainly knew me . . . but how well did she know Bill?

About six months later, I was at a party in Santa Monica at the home of a songwriter friend. There were many interesting, artistic people in the group and I happened to strike up a conversation with a woman who was a docent at a local museum.

Madelyn said, "I have the greatest guy for you. His name is Bill and he lives up the street in Malibu. He

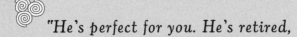

"He's perfect for you. He's retired,

Irish, and very good-looking.

Can I give him your number?"

broke up with a woman in Carmel a few months ago and is definitely ready to start dating."

This was too weird. Could it be the same Bill?

If my dear friend in Carmel and a complete stranger in Santa Monica both thought this Bill and I were perfect for each other, it had to be magic.

Madelyn gave Bill my number.

"Do you remember me?" I asked when he called a few days later. "Peg in Carmel suggested we meet a few months ago."

"Yeah. Vaguely," Bill answered.

"So, we really need to get together since both Northern and Southern California think we're a match." My voice rang with enthusiasm.

Bill suggested a lovely beachfront restaurant. We ate, chatted, and decided that our mutual friends had no idea what we were looking for in a partner. Bill loved horse racing, road trips, and preferred blondes. I loved cruises and could care less about the color of a man's hair or even if he has any. I do care about how shallow someone is, though. I shortly figured out that Bill's dating demands were about an inch deep when he asked me how many dates I usually go on before I sleep with a man. To his credit, we were talking about how dating had changed from when we were in our twenties.

It was a good lunch and great scenery. Nothing lost. Nothing gained.

I went home, called Peg, and read her the newest version of my revised *Personal Perfect Man List*.

> *Note:* Destiny is not always
> what you want.

Date Twenty-Three

Wine with the Whiner
"Chad"

I was wallowing in loneliness. My salvation was buttered popcorn, nachos, and Lifetime Television. But all the days and nights of introspection and overeating did finally bring me to an astonishing revelation. The list of men I had been dating had names used in a bygone era: Seymour, Morris, Leonard, Bernie, Jerry, Albert, Morey. These were names of men who were born before 1935. I had to find some happening guys with names like Justin, Josh, Preston, or Matt. Even if a Seymour was born in 1950, he probably was predestined to wear glasses and be an optometrist. What picture does Morris conjure up in your mind? Now, what does Chad, Ian, Damon, or Jeff do for you? Much better. I like that image.

It was again time to broaden my search for a life partner. I read *L.A. Weekly* and quickly saw that most of the men in that periodical's personal ads had names like Chip, Buck, and Swami and were looking for either other guys with names like Rock or Troy or for a threesome with Bambi, Shanika, and Ginger. Enough with *L.A. Weekly!*

Next, I investigated online romantic chat rooms. Instead of looking in the "over fifty" category, I decided to peruse some younger groups. It was there that I found Chad and Edward.

Chad and I started to email and he sounded great, as so many had in their notes. He was a lawyer whose hobby was wine. I pretended that I had some knowledge on the subject when, in fact, I couldn't tell a merlot from a Beaujolais. Basically, my knowledge about wine-tasting was that you sip, hold, swirl, and spit; a task I had learned years before in Bounne, France, where I also pretended to enjoy the subtleties of the grape.

"What more did I need to know?
The man liked to shop."

Chad and I met at a little bar in Malibu on a Thursday night. Apparently, Thursday was the new Saturday. The place was charming, small, and very chic. I had not talked to Chad on the phone, which was definitely against my rules of Internet dating, but I had a great feeling about him from his emails. He sounded smart. Our online notes ranged from the mundane to deep conversations about our mutual love for Nordstrom over Bloomingdales and our passion for animals. What more did I need to know? The man liked to shop.

Chad walked in. He was five feet, three inches, one hundred and seventeen pounds, with a nose that must have been the appendage that pushed him over the one hundred mark. Once I got past the realization that he looked like an elf from Italy, there was his voice. He didn't speak, he whined.

"Do you like red or white wine better?" he asked in a singsong voice.

"It depends on what I'm eating." I thought my answer was intelligent and correct.

"I'm talking in generalities." He continued in a voice that was an octave above mine. "You don't have to get persnickety about it. Here, try this syrah. Then we'll move on to a pinot noir and then maybe a dessert brandy."

I didn't want the syrah or chardonnay or the pinot or any other wine. I wanted a Diet Coke with a lemon and the date to be over.

"Listen," he whined, "I think we can learn to like each other. I'm going to Napa next weekend. Why don't you join me? Separate rooms, of course. It's the thirty-seventh anniversary of the first American bottle of pink champagne. It's going to be just so much fun. I have a client who imports . . . "

I politely turned the Napa invitation down and made it through way too many stories about Chad's clients and way too many glasses of wine. My head was spinning from the entire night. *Learn to like each other?* Like is not a studied subject in school but an instinct deep within us. I bumped into my neighbor, Bronwyn, as I was getting into my condo elevator and shared that I'd just had a date with a guy who sounded like Gilbert Gottfried.

"Oh, was it Chad Rosenstein?"

She was right. I learned that Chad was twenty-two years younger than me and had struck out with just about every Jewish single female on the west side of Los Angeles between the ages of thirty and sixty, including my very informative neighbor.

Note: The fruit of the grape may be sweet but whiners hit a sour note.

Ascot and Accent
"Edward"

On to Edward. This time, I insisted we chat on the phone. To my delight, Edward had a beautiful highborn British accent. I found myself saying things like *bloody well* and *brilliant*. It seems that when I talk to a Brit, I become a sponge and take on the lilt of the language. Men from England sound so well-heeled and successful. Edward was no exception. Maybe he was a displaced duke or lord, or a gentleman who played polo alongside Charles. My mind was creating a fantasy of winters at our mansion outside of London and summers by the sea. I would shop

> *"My mind was creating a fantasy of winters at our mansion outside of London and summers by the sea."*

at Harrods while he had his cravats custom made on Seville Road. We would meet for high tea at the Ritz, enjoy a concert at Royal Albert Hall, followed by dinner at The Savoy Grill. Ascot was just one dream away.

After several chats that were so surface you could roller-skate on them, Edward asked me to meet him at the Stage deli in Beverly Hills. I was hoping for the Polo Lounge at the Beverly Hills Hotel, but pastrami on rye would do.

It was noon when the hostess escorted me to the table where Edward was already seated. There he was, around seventy years old and wearing a heavy tweed jacket and ascot. It was July and ninety-two degrees out. Over matzo ball soup, I learned that Edward was an unemployed baker who had been living on disability since he burned his hand trying to rescue a burning brioche. He was looking for a woman to support him and thought his accent and ascot were enough to close the deal. At least he was honest. I picked up the check and said ta ta, leaving my dreams of cricket with our neighbor Fergie and tea with Elton in my empty soup bowl.

Note: Patty-cake, patty-cake,
baker's man, if he's a moocher,
run as fast as you can.

Stud Muffin Two
"Matt"

". . . and I'm looking for a woman between fifty and ninety-nine."

What a strange profile. Usually men in their forties are trying to date women in their twenties or thirties. What was wrong with this man? Ninety-nine? Oh well, at least my age was on the low side of his search.

I emailed Cameraman413 with the usual inquiry.

"Hi, Cameraman. Saw your profile and it seemed interesting. Take a look at mine and if you like what you see, email me back." By now, I had written those three sentences hundreds of times.

What I really wanted to ask was, *Why the hell do you want to date an old broad? Do you look like Quasimodo? Do you have three eyes?*

The response came in three hours.

"Yes, your profile looks very interesting. We're in the same business. Okay, I know you're going to ask about the age thing. Basically, I like older women. Just got out of a ten-year relationship with a woman who was twelve years older than me. Women past fifty don't want children. I have one and that's enough. They also are clear in what they want in a relationship. No games. Let's talk. I'm working on a film right now, so late evening is best. 818-524-5 . . . "

I wrote down Matt's phone number but wasn't convinced I would call. The whole idea of again dating a younger man was questionable. There was a child in the mix. That could cause complications. On the other hand, the thought of young energy again was exciting. Since Matt didn't put his actual age in his profile, I was concerned he might be one of those weirdos who are really just twenty and want to taunt older women. I had been teased by several kids who probably got off by giving an old lady a fantasy that just wasn't going to happen.

Rationalizing that it was just a phone call and my time, I decided to call the next evening.

Matt's voice sounded like a professional newsman's, deep and strong. I knew I wasn't dealing with a teaser or child here. We talked for at least two hours, mostly about our personal histories . . . where we grew up, schooling, jobs. I gave Matt my number.

The next night was a repeat. But this time, we talked for three hours, mostly about our "now" . . . likes, pet peeves, interests. There was never a lack of conversation. Words and thoughts flowed easily. And, everything I heard, I liked.

He asked interesting questions. "What's in front of you right now?"

"I'm in the living room and I'm looking at a small box that one of my son's gave me."

"What does it look like?"

"It's porcelain, white and pink and says *Never Settle for Less Than You Deserve*. Nice saying."

"Your son gives lovely gifts and good advice."

Night three, Matt called, as he promised, around eight in the evening.

"I just got home and I'm beat. I'm working sixteen-hour days for the next few weeks."

"That's a grueling schedule," I answered, to show understanding.

"I'd love to meet you, but I'm not sure when that can happen. Even working over the weekend." I didn't think Matt was brushing me off. He did sound tired.

"Why don't I drive out to the Valley and we can just have some coffee?"

"You would do that? Great. When?"

"How about now?" I had decided I really wanted to meet this man.

I threw on some jeans, a T-shirt, and a black silk bomber jacket and drove a half hour to the Encino Starbucks on Ventura. There sat Matt wearing jeans, a T-shirt, and a black silk bomber jacket. We looked like a pair of mall-walker twins. Serendipity?

I scrutinized my blind date.

Height: About six feet two.

Weight: Too much. Big double chin with a belly to match.

Hair: Gray and long enough to put in a ponytail.

*"It was one of the best kisses
I'd ever had. There was something
about this man that turned me on,
double chin and all."*

Hands: Large.

Feet: At least a size thirteen.

Face: Sweet.

Eyes: Blue and caring.

I wasn't attracted physically to Matt, but liked what I was hearing. He was a cameraman, mostly doing special effects. He had worked on many films and had lots of stories to share. He wasn't aggressive or shy. He was relaxed and self-assured. He listened as I talked and asked questions.

"It's almost eleven and you have to be up in six hours for work." I couldn't believe how fast the time had gone.

Matt walked me to my car.

"Can I see you again?" he asked in a soft voice.

Before I could answer, he bent down and kissed me. When he saw that I wasn't resisting, he kissed me again, and my attraction to Matt began.

It was one of the best kisses I'd ever had. I felt a surge of energy from my head to my toes. There was something about this man that turned me on, double chin and all.

Matt was ten years younger than me. He had been divorced for about seven years and was concentrating on his career. In contrast to Stud Muffin Mike, this man had goals.

He had partial custody of his thirteen-year-old daughter. He adored his child. His face lit up when he talked about her.

I started to see Matt every chance he could get free. It would sometimes be ten o'clock at night, after he finished the day's shoot.

"I'm just leaving the set. Want me to drop by?"

The good in this relationship was that we really liked each other. We became fast friends and had a true interest in each other's lives. We talked for hours on end.

The bad: Matt and I were on different economic planes and timelines. At forty-five, he didn't own a home, his work was sporadic, and his ability to travel was nil. He always had to be close by for a work call. His dream was to become a producer, which would afford him the lifestyle he wanted. He would be working for the next fifteen years.

I don't think I ever went on a "date" with Matt. It was always coming over to my house or grabbing a bite to eat on the way to the Directors Guild for a free film screening. There were never weekends away. There were never flowers, love notes, or gifts. But for some reason, I liked having Matt around.

He would go on location for weeks at a time and never call. There would be an occasional email but that was about it. I was content to play with my girlfriends and fend for myself socially. I sometimes got upset when I didn't hear from him but remembered we had no commitment. He wasn't my husband or fiancé. We were free agents.

Actually, it was while seeing Matt that I turned a corner and began to really enjoy my date-free time. I went to lots of plays in Los Angeles's small equity waiver theaters with my friend Erica. I flew to Florida and went boating with my opera singer friend Melody. I went to New York to visit relatives. I went on a cruise with my buddy Janet. I visited my children. I sat home and watched Oprah. I learned to make a beef Wellington. I sponge-painted my powder room.

Finally, I was learning how to create my own life. Whether it was Matt's confidence in me or time, I was beginning to feel strong.

I was always happy when Matt came back into town and we resumed seeing each other. But I didn't pine away the hours waiting. Our relationship was basically a good friendship, with sex. If anyone had told me ten years previously that I would have a sexual relationship with someone I wasn't madly in love with, I would have told them they were crazy. I wasn't in love with Matt; I was in like. The sex was good. We talked about each other's needs. He was a considerate lover and made sure I was satisfied. He held me, he told me how wonderful I was, we pleased each other, and we played. It was uncomplicated.

I didn't have the sexual tension with Matt that I'd had with Stud Muffin Mike. There were no clothes being ripped off in the hall or sex on the beach.

With Matt, it was all about caring.

We made a pact. In five years, if neither of us was married or in a serious relationship, we would move in together. We both didn't want to grow old alone.

But about a year or so into our relationship, I realized that like wasn't enough for me. I sensed there would be no "us" in our future. So, while still seeing Matt, I went back online to find love.

Note: Communication is sexy . . .
both in bed and while eating
beef Wellington.

Lights, Camera, Love
"Scott"

I pinched myself over and over again. I was in love.

It didn't take long to realize that Scott was a special man.

Age: One year older than me.

Occupation: Television director, working.

Height: Five feet ten.

Weight: A little chubby.

Hair: Plenty of curly brown.

Cultural background: A nice Jewish boy.

Style in clothing: Horrible.

Personality: Adorable, kind, funny.

By our third date, we were making out like high school sweethearts. By our sixth, we had proved that all the parts not only worked but fit together just beautifully. I would lie next to Scott's furry body, nestled in his arms and silently attest that I was the luckiest woman alive.

We connected on Match.com. A friend dared him to join and I, by now, was an Internet-dating regular. I scanned the new men on a weekly basis, often taking the initiative. After emailing and chatting a few times on the phone, we finally met for lunch at a restaurant in the Valley. That month the poundage was down, so I wore a red low-cut T-shirt, jeans, a navy blazer, and high-heeled boots. I felt strong and in control.

Scott and I both seemed pleasantly surprised at our blind date luck. Apparently, he had met some rather strange women during his Internet-dating experience. About the time he was successfully impressing me with the long list of hit television shows he had directed, I heard my name being called from across the room.

"Fancy meeting you here." My good friend Nanci was talking to me but staring at my male lunch partner.

"Scott and I both seemed
pleasantly suprised by our
blind date luck."

"Nanci, this is Scott Miller. What brings you to
this side of the hill?"

"Business lunch." She paused. "Scott Miller?"
Nanci's brain was spinning. "Aren't you a director?"

"Yes."

"Did you ever work on one of Andy Griffith's
shows?"

"Yes," Scott answered with a smirk on his face. He
had worked on most of them.

"Then you knew my dad. He was the producer. I
knew your name was familiar. In fact, you must know
my brother. He costarred on the . . ."

I wasn't needed. Nanci and Scott just strolled down
memory lane until her business associate finally arrived.
As she left for her table, she gave me one of those not-
so-subtle "good job" winks, which was seen by Scott
and everyone else in the restaurant.

Two and a half hours later, Scott and I were still talking, amazed at what we had in common.

"This might be too forward and I know it's last minute, but I have tickets for the King Tut exhibit tomorrow. Would you like to join me?"

I accepted, and there started our romance.

For months, I saw Scott several times a week. He called almost every day and always showed up at my door with flowers or candy or a gift for my newly adopted pound dog, Bijoux. I was falling hard for this sweet man. I visited the set of the television drama he was directing and was introduced to the crew and actors with pride. I was Scott's girl and everyone knew it. I sat on the set and beamed as my director honey called the shots. He was so talented.

So, why was this nice looking, very eligible man available? I soon learned details of his one and only marriage. He knew on his honeymoon that a mistake had been made. His wife showed signs of deep psychological problems. They had a son early on and two years later, a daughter. By their sixth anniversary, Scott knew he could not stay in a loveless, confused marriage. He moved out but only for a week. A deal was made and he again moved back home. A second floor was added; there would be no marital relations and he would live in the house and see his children grow up. She got full financial support and Scott got to be a full-time dad.

This arrangement apparently lasted for seventeen years, until the last child went off to college.

I was Scott's first serious relationship since his divorce became final. I could tell he was uncomfortable getting close to a woman. In every possible way, I tried to make him feel safe and appreciated.

But, I was also honest about my needs. On about our fifth date, Scott asked me what I wanted long-term.

"My ultimate goal would be to have a full-time companion, possibly a marriage."

I never minced words. I was always up-front.

When I asked Scott what he wanted, the answer was always vague or noncommittal.

"I don't know. I guess I'll just have to wait and see."

I knew early on that Scott hadn't dated very much

since his divorce. It became evident that the actual act of lovemaking wasn't that important to him. We had sex, but that's not what our relationship was being based on. Once the excitement of having a new partner wore off, sex became secondary to warm hugs, snuggles, and kisses with an occasional Saturday night roll in the hay. In spite of my periodical libido frustrations, I really wanted to make this relationship work. I wanted to be with this man.

Our friends were as different as Scott's and my lifestyles. Scott enjoyed simple folk, educated people who were not complicated. He liked to eat at HomeTown Buffet and other restaurants where going up for thirds and fourths was not only expected but considered a birthright. Most of his friends had homes with a ham radio tower in the backyard. Ham radios? I thought that was a dying hobby that only old, lonely people participated in. My friends usually didn't eat ham, listened mostly to FM radio, and only did buffets on movie sets or cruises.

My idea of a lovely weekend with Scott was to drive up to Carmel or Santa Barbara, leisurely walk through art galleries, and dine on chocolate-covered strawberries, brie, and pâté in front of a roaring fireplace in our hotel room. We did several of those trips and they were absolutely magical.

Then there were the getaways that Scott looked forward to . . . like the California Ham Radio Convention in Fresno. We stayed at a Holiday Inn and ate hot dogs all weekend with men and women who wore bibbed jeans.

I met his children.

He met my children.

We spent holidays together.

I accepted our differences.

He worried about our differences.

But neither of us said, "I love you."

I couldn't remember the last time I was so content. There was something about this man that made me smile from ear to ear. He made me feel safe and wanted. Our relationship was easy. Scott Miller was my boyfriend.

"I love you."

We were in the shower at the Ritz-Carlton in San Juan, Puerto Rico . . . on a vacation that was my holiday gift to Scott. The words just came blurting out as I scrubbed his back. It was Valentine's weekend and, in my heart and mind, I thought Scott might propose.

"I love you," I said again. I wanted to hear those words back. I would have been happy with "You are so special to me." But there was silence.

I let the water hide my tears.

My hurt permeated the air. I dressed and started to pack.

"Don't leave. I'll take the next flight back," Scott said as he watched me throw clothes into my bag.

"I know how much you love cruises. This is ridiculous." Scott tried to smooth things over. We were scheduled to board a ship in two days and he realized I was serious about leaving.

I spoke through my tears. "I don't want to go on the cruise alone and I certainly don't want to be with someone as frozen as you. I know you love me. Tell me."

Scott was silent for at least a minute and then said in a low voice, "I can't."

I left the room and walked along the beach. My heart was broken and I knew our relationship was over. It would not be the *forever after* I had dreamed.

Scott convinced me that we should stay on the trip and take the cruise. Maybe things could be worked out.

We talked, we danced, we slept in the same bed and even made love. Instead of the proposal I had fantasized about for Valentine's Day, there was perfume. As hard as Scott tried to be attentive, I knew that what we had was temporary. This man had been hurt badly by another woman and I was paying for his fear.

It was a year and a half I'd never forget. I ached when it ended. The phone calls stopped. The borrowed CDs were returned and the drawer in each other's homes was emptied.

About six months after Scott and I broke up, I received an email from him. In the subject line was "My new girlfriend." *How odd,* I thought. *He's sending me a picture of the new woman in his life?* When I opened the attachment, I found an adorable picture of Polly, a mixed-breed puppy he'd adopted from a shelter.

"See, I was able to commit to a girl. I'll work on telling her she's loved."

Note: You usually can't fix what has been broken for twenty-three years.

Liar, Liar, Pants on Fire
"Blake"

Breaking up with Scott left me feeling empty. My ego was shot and now my trust in the opposite sex had been sorely tested. I told myself that this was probably what some divorced people must feel. The person you love is still out there but doesn't want you. All Scott wanted was his freedom, a dog, his own bed, and a large radio tower.

For months, I holed up watching television, playing old songs on the piano, gaining weight, and pining for Scott. Then one Wednesday night, while watching *When Harry Met Sally* for the fourth time, I realized that I really wanted what Meg Ryan had. And I'm not referring to just the restaurant scene. I wanted a best friend, lover, and companion.

I was ready to date again.

So back online I went and met Blake.

Barnes & Noble, 7:30 PM in the Starbucks coffee shop. I was looking for a tall, dark-haired man who was eight years my junior and worked for a think tank.

There he was . . . a vision for my lonely eyes. In a black turtleneck and slacks, Blake looked exactly like I had dreamed he would. He was six feet three and had a great body and thick, dark hair with just a few sprinkles of gray. We talked for about an hour.

"I work for Global Mind Source solving problems for the government in the area of intelligence. That's all I can really say, except my work takes me all over the world."

It sounded so romantic. So dangerous. My own James Bond.

Blake ended our date with a pat on my back and a request to see me again. I happily accepted.

"Peg, this guy is adorable. He's sophisticated, he's intelligent. He's taking me to a foreign film tomorrow night."

"Go slow, sweetie. And be careful. Remember what happened at the last foreign film date you had." Peg was always trying to protect my heart.

The movie was dark and brooding but Blake loved it. I hated it. Afterward, we went to Kate Matilini, an L.A. hot spot, and sat next to some famous rap star who had an entourage the size of Pittsburgh.

"I don't understand this rap singing," Blake said, looking over at the group next to us. "It's not singing. It's not poetry. What is it?"

"I disagree, Blake. It is poetry. Just not always rhyming and not always about subjects we understand."

Out of nowhere, Blake leaned over and kissed me.

"This is what you do to me."

As he spoke, he took my hand and placed it on his crotch under the table. Supposedly, he had an erection. Before I pulled my hand away, I felt something the size of a small walnut and concluded that Blake was tall but had a teeny weenie.

In spite of, or maybe subconsciously because of, his lewd conduct, we dated for the next several months. My interest in him was waning but something about this man fascinated me. Was he a "bad boy"? Was he the type who flirted but didn't know how to have an intimate relationship?

There were walks on the beach, a visit to the Museum of Contemporary Art—Los Angeles, more foreign films, visits to book stores where he showed me naked pictures of men and women in the name of art, and dinners at my place. We had long talks about politics and music. There were kisses. But there was no sex. Blake was certainly unusual. He had never been married but said there had been several long relationships. He hardly ever talked about work but drove me by his office in Santa Monica several times and pointed out his window in the high-rise.

"It's time we meet this man. We'll be at the condo in Palm Desert over the weekend. Bring him down. Are you guys sharing a bedroom?" Prim and proper Peg snickered.

"No. He's really strange when it comes to sex. He lights the fire but never hoses it down. We'll come down just for the day."

"Okay. Up to you," Peg answered.

"It's just nice to have someone to have dinner with who can carry on an intelligent conversation. You know what I mean, Peg?"

"Sure. He doesn't turn you on!"

"Or I don't turn him on." I really wondered if that was the case.

"Another subject," Peg countered. "Still playing tennis?"

"Yeah, I'm taking lessons and Blake said he played on his college team. Should we plan on doubles?"

"Bad back, but I'll arrange some lessons for you guys with our pro."

I sat on the bench as my date slammed the ball back and sometimes forth with the gorgeous tennis club teacher. Blake's form reminded me of an uncoordinated ape, flinging his arms above his head while lumbering to try and hit the next oncoming ball. His racket was at least thirty years old . . . wooden and small. It was probably the same one he used in college. He wore orange plaid shorts and a navy dress shirt. I, on the other hand, had on crisp white shorts, a white collared polo shirt, and twirled a new graphite Prince.

As I mentally summarized the inconsistency of Blake's story of brilliant college tennis with the vision before me, I noticed his billfold on the bench next to me. My own desire to become Jane Bond was overwhelming. I carefully scooped it up and threw it in my purse. Even if he'd looked over, Blake would never have been able to see me looking through his wallet.

First was his license. He was three years younger than me, not eight.

Second, he lied about where he lived. I had never been to his home, which supposedly was in Santa Monica. He lived in Torrance, easily twenty miles south and a far less exclusive address. Lastly, tucked behind his license was a current unemployment slip. The teeny weenie didn't have a job. I carefully slipped the wallet back on the bench, trying to contain the anger that had consumed my body.

It took all I had to be polite and smile through dinner with Peg and Buzz. I told Peg of my findings before we went out and she cleverly tried to entrap Blake with questions about work and life in general. Blake didn't budge from his story. He worked at Global Mind Source and lived in Santa Monica.

There was no trust left in me and I never intended to see this loser again. Knowing there were probably more secrets hidden inside this devious man, I decided to spy more and get some sweet, juicy revenge.

Computers are wonderful. If you know what you're doing, you can sometimes follow a person around, see what chat rooms they are in, and, by using a name they are not familiar with, get some real dirt.

I became Latetia31, Spongegirl40, SexySister103, and PartyAnimal715.

From room to room, I followed Blake and listened to his chats. He hit on me, of course, thinking I was a thirty-one-year-old divorced woman from Atlanta.

He talked about all his sexual conquests and how he was such a stud in bed. He bragged about his prowess and taunted females with filthy, vulgar talk, saying he would fly anywhere to give them pleasure. He promised orgasms beyond a woman's wildest dreams and sexual satisfaction better than any battery toy could provide.

Blake had many more problems than simply lying about his age and employment. Blake was the man you report to the Internet watchdogs . . . which I did.

Revenge? As SexySister103, I met Blake at Dutton's Bookstore in Brentwood. I stood there with an eleven-by-seventeen sign that read GOTCHA.

I guess those who can't deliver, talk. I now understand why sex was never part of our relationship.

It sickened me to know I had dated a man who pretended to be what he was not. I was finished. No more dating.

I needed and wanted to be by myself.

Note: When I was a kid, our housekeeper, Anna May King, told me not to trust a liar further than I can spit. I was learning how to expectorate like a lady, inch by inch.

Hey, Girlfriend
"Joan"

When you look for things to do, it can lead to social relationships. My focus was now to enjoy life being single and to mingle with friends, old and new. I joined a gym near my home called Women's Power and worked out several times a week. That's how I met Joan.

She was in her early fifties, had a great body for her age, and kept it that way by exercising at least five times a week. Joan didn't have one ounce of fat on her. I was so jealous. Her hair was short and blonde and her blue eyes were always enhanced by mascara, lining, and shadow. She always had makeup on, even in the sauna.

We talked while on the treadmill, complained while doing weights, and chatted while cooling down at the juice bar.

"You know, this women's lecture group I belong to meets every Wednesday night, seven o'clock. Usually pretty interesting and lots of fun people. Would you like to go with me? Potluck." Joan was very casual about the invitation.

"I'd love to, Joan. Give me the details and I'll meet you there. I have a dentist appointment and I'm not sure what time I'll finish."

Joan wrote down the information, including her cell phone number in case I got lost.

I wasn't comfortable attending functions where I didn't know most of the people, but Joan was nice and it was time to broaden my circle of friends.

I pulled up to the Hollywood Hills home right on time, hoping my friend would be there to soften my solo entrance.

"Hey, so glad you could make it. Let me introduce you around." I was relieved Joan seemed to know the entire group. "This is Boots, Jill, Harriet, Janine, and Patty. I'll introduce you to the others later. Want a drink?"

"Not yet. Thanks." I put my pasta salad down near the other potluck offerings and began to mingle.

The room was filled with around thirty rather attractive women of all ages. They were laughing, eating, and chatting away. By their body language, it looked like most knew each other. I figured this must be a weekly night out without husbands or boyfriends.

The lecture began. The talk was entitled "A Lesbian's Right to Adopt . . . " I expected something a little more mainstream like "Sexual Harassment in the Workplace," but found the speaker and subject matter informative and interesting.

For a fleeting moment, I suspected that the group might be gay, but pushed that out of my mind thinking, *Why would I have been invited?*

Over the following month, Joan and I met several times a week for dinners, sometimes followed by a movie. I was comfortable with my new friend. She was smart and funny. I learned that she had been in only two long-term relationships of five years each and had never been married. I didn't ask why. Not my business.

There were always little hugs when we said goodbye. Sometimes, a peck on the cheek. Hello and goodbye hugs and kisses are part of my girlfriend routine.

I love having close female friends. You can talk to other women about everything from blackheads to hot flashes and they understand. I talked to Joan a lot about my dating fiascoes and how I was enjoying moving forward without worrying about finding a man.

"Why don't we go on a cruise together?" Joan asked as we finished up our dinner at Gaucho Grill in Brentwood.

I was surprised by this invitation that seemed to come out of nowhere. "I adore cruises. I certainly will consider it. When do you have in mind? Where?"

"Oh, I don't know. How about next week? Caribbean." Joan smiled as we left the restaurant.

"You've got to be kidding. So fast? I doubt we'd find a cabin." I was used to planning cruises months ahead.

"There's a special cruise sailing from Ft. Lauderdale that has some space. But I have to tell you, the whole ship has been bought out by Olivia, a gay tour organization. It goes to Key West, Jamaica, Cozumel, and back to Ft. Lauderdale."

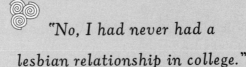

"No, I had never had a lesbian relationship in college."

"Why would I want to go on a gay cruise?" I was confused by Joan's suggestion.

"Because you and I are lesbians."

I stood outside the restaurant speechless. Had I given Joan the wrong message? I tried to flash back to every minute I had spent with her and concluded that I had not led her on. What was she thinking?

"Joan, I had some suspicions you might be gay, but I'm definitely straight. You know that, right?"

"I know you were married. That doesn't mean a thing. You like me; we get along great. I feel there could be something between us more meaningful. Just think about it. It might be an eye-opening experience for you. You never had a fling in college?"

No, I had never had a lesbian relationship in college. But, I did think about her offer and her. In fact, I fantasized about being with this beautiful woman. She did have full lips that looked kissable. She was very sexy and I imagined what it would be like to hold her in my arms. But when it came right down to thinking about being intimate with my new friend, my mind just couldn't go there.

I was not gay, or even bi.

We met a few days later for lunch, this time at California Pizza Kitchen.

"I'm very flattered, Joan, but this old gal is set in her ways. I like men. I like the smell of a man, all the parts of a man, the sound and touch of a man. I really did think about what it would be like being with a woman, you know, romantically, and it just didn't work. You know I adore you, but as a friend."

"I was sure you were gay. Just not out yet. Damn. I'm usually right on the money."

Joan hugged me and left.

"See you soon?" I yelled as she walked toward her car. I didn't want our friendship to end.

But I no longer saw Joan at the gym. I went at all different times of day hoping to bump into her. I left phone messages, but she didn't answer my invitations for lunch.

> *Note:* Whether straight or gay,
> go after the one you want.

Laughless, Late
"Elliott"

It had been almost a year and a half since I had gone out on a date. I worked. I played. I didn't seek the company of men. Then one day, as I was loading some shopping bags into my car, I saw a couple holding hands while they walked along Rodeo Drive, laughing as they window-shopped. They never let go of each other, like they were two people joined at the fingers.

The pangs of wanting to be with someone again came back and I decided to revisit my old standby . . . online dating. All the insecurities of this process of mate selection returned. I combed the sites and posted profiles. Within two days, I had three "hits" and I made a date with Elliott. Our meeting place would be The House of Pancakes, 8 PM, Thursday night.

I arrived at 7:55 PM and entered the restaurant looking for a forty-seven-year-old male who was looking for a fifty-seven-year-old woman. No one approached. But, as I scanned the twenty or so booths, all sticky with syrup, I noticed a man seated alone. Certain he was my date, I walked over to his table and sat down.

"Hello, Elliott, I'm Sherry." I reached out my hand for him to welcome me.

He looked up slowly.

"I'm not Elliott." The poor man looked at me in disbelief. A total stranger was seated opposite him.

I was horrified and apologized several times as I backed away, almost bowing. I made my way out of the restaurant to the parking lot and my car. I should have surmised that a man seated at a table with silver dollars and hash browns in front of him was not waiting for a date.

"I have to get out of here." I was talking aloud to myself. By the fourth time around the block, I con-

> *"I was horrified and apologized several times as I backed away, almost bowing."*

vinced myself that I could not go back in the restaurant and should just blow the date off. There was a nearby In-N-Out Burger place that I headed to, fully intending to demolish a Double-Double cheeseburger and fries. But before entering the drive-through, I felt sufficiently guilty to head back to The House of Pancakes. I could not stand someone up.

I sucked in my breath and pride and again entered the pancake eatery. This time, a man approached me and offered his hand. At the same time, Mr. Mistake At The Table came up to him, slapped him on the back, and said, "Hi Elliott. How ya doing?" He then put his arm around my shoulder and proceeded to tell Elliott what a great woman he was about to meet. I couldn't stop laughing. And poor Elliott, he was totally confused.

After we sat down and before I realized what a bore he was, I told him of my mistaken identity incident.

Elliott didn't laugh. He didn't think the fiasco was funny. He apologized for being fifteen minutes late and ended our date by saying our personalities were too dissimilar for us to be a match.

For me, the funniest thing about the entire evening was the fact that as I looked at Mr. Mistake standing next to me, I realized that he couldn't have been more than twenty-eight years old. Now, that's being delusional!

> *Note:* It's nice to fantasize but don't
> bring innocents into your dreams.

Work. I will work and forget about dating. I spent the next year producing concerts for world-renowned tenor Giorgio Aristo and soprano Melody Kielisch. I felt good about myself. I was having fun. I was doing something creative and that I enjoyed. Actually, something that I loved. Giorgio had been my friend since childhood and his beautiful, talented wife, Melody, and I became fast friends. I saw my company's name in lights at Lincoln Center. I sold out 2,000-seat auditoriums. I was riding high on success. I was good as a producer.

I had nary a date.

At first, the success seemed lonely. I wanted to have someone in the audience who was unselfishly happy for me and who understood the achievement. It wasn't about the money or the accolades. It was about the pride of accomplishment. "Look, Ma, I made it to Broadway." But Ma wasn't around and Warren wasn't around.

It was Melody who convinced me that the accomplishment was mine alone and that I should be happy for myself. Eventually, I began to own and enjoy my success.

The tour wound down. There were no more posters to design and no more commercials to create. It was time to go back to Los Angeles and think about my future. What did I want to do next?

R.O.M. Strike Three
"Len"

Sometimes, when you least expect it, lightening strikes, again.

Ring.

"Do you know who this is?"

I hate it when people play the name-guessing game.

"Len, is that you? You sound so different. How have you been?"

"Funny you should ask."

Len had just returned home from a three-week stay at Cedars-Sinai Medical Center in Los Angeles where a brain tumor had been successfully removed.

"All the time I was laying there, I only thought of you. You, you're the one for me. Aren't you flattered?"

"That's very sweet, Len."

"Come over for dinner tomorrow night. I really want to see you."

Something was different. His voice wasn't sluggish and he didn't sound like he was doped up on antidepressants and tranquilizers. He sounded clear, coherent, and to my amazement, likeable.

"I'll have dinner with you, as a friend." I couldn't believe I was saying that.

"I knew you still loved me, baby."

The next night, I drove to Brentwood and had dinner with the Rich Old Man, who welcomed me at the door in purple silk pajamas and a matching bathrobe. He looked like Barney, the dinosaur. His male nurse took my coat and retreated to the kitchen to have dinner with the chauffeur while the cook served us in the dining room.

Apparently, the tumor had been growing for years and the doctors attributed his depression and strange mood swings to his illness. Maybe there was a new Len to be discovered . . . a kinder, caring Len.

For the next month, I dined at Chez Lenny twice a week. After an early dinner, we settled in on the leather couch in the screening room and either watched satellite TV from New York or the latest DVDs.

At about week two, Len introduced the following information:

"You know, part of my drug therapy is taking testosterone." He winked at me, which I ignored. "I'm seventy-one but have the urges of a thirty-year-old. I can get it up in five minutes. Just wait, you'll see."

I sat there in silence. This man was bragging about his penis. Maybe he had another tumor they hadn't removed. A normal man doesn't talk that way.

"I could get young chicks up here all day long if I wanted. My nurse has connections. But those young ones just want to fuck me for my money. You, you want to fuck me because you love me."

"I don't love you, Len. We have a history. That's all. You had better behave yourself."

"You'll love me again. Just wait and see."

After every dinner, I was shown to the door at eight o'clock. The master of the house went to sleep very early still and didn't vary his routine for anyone.

This was getting boring. I refused more invitations to dine at his home.

So, two weeks later, when Len invited me to have dinner with him at The Four Seasons Hotel, I accepted. This would be his first big outing since being home from the hospital. The chauffeur dropped us off and I took it from there. Len was still unstable on his feet. His eyesight and gait had been altered by the surgery and he listed a bit to the right. It was like driving a large old car that didn't have power steering. I held his arm and guided him into the elegant restaurant of this exclusive hotel.

To our left sat a beautiful couple holding hands and speaking in German. To our right sat the even-more-gorgeous-in-real-life Brad Pitt and a male friend or business associate. There were candles on the tables and a violin played discretely in the background.

Waving a lamb chop in his left hand, Len spoke.

"Two million. I've upped my offer to two million, but you still only get twenty-five thousand a year for clothes." This big man's voice was booming. "Did I tell you that my dick works just fine now? Look at all these young men in the room. They'd like a dick like mine. Marry me and you'll get two mil and a gigantic, working dick!"

I sat there, shrinking slowly in my chair, too embarrassed to move and too shocked to realize that the entire room, including Mr. Pitt, was staring our way. Within twenty minutes of ordering dinner, this insane man had again proposed to me and notified the crème de la crème of Beverly Hills that his penis was in fine working order.

When I gained my composure, I summoned the waiter, had Mr. Rich Old Man pay the check, called the chauffeur on my cell, and sent Lenny on his horny way, never to be seen or heard from again.

Note: When their three strikes are up, they're out for good.

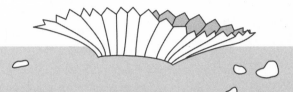

Stud Muffin One . . . And Again
"Mike"

I remembered Stud Muffin Mike as always having perfect romantic timing. He somehow knew when I would be thinking about taking the old vibrator out of the bathroom drawer and would call to invite himself over.

His timing could not have been better when he called after six years of silence. I was out of work, bored with life, and bored with Los Angeles.

"So, what have you been up to?" I was so curious if he had a new job or a new wife.

"Not much. Doing the same stuff. Not married. Are you seeing anyone?"

"No, definitely not." I kicked myself for not being more evasive.

"Then how about dinner? Thursday night?"

"Sure. It will be great to see you."

I was so excited. After all, Mike was my first sexual partner after my husband died and we had remarkable chemistry. I needed some razzle-dazzle in my life. It had been a long time since I had been out of breath from anything besides running on my treadmill.

Mike showed up looking fantastic, wearing jeans, a pink polo shirt, and sandals. He had lost about thirty pounds and his new muscles bulged from under his short sleeves. His thick black hair had lots more gray, and he was wearing rimless glasses.

"How long has it been?" He was the first to speak, ending the awkward moment. "Your place looks pretty much the same."

"I have new carpet. Nice seeing you, too." I checked my body and mind for any signs of excitement. To my amazement, my heart wasn't fluttering. I didn't want to rip off his clothes like I used to, and I definitely didn't want to jump his bones.

We found a few things to talk about in the car and

over dinner . . . like my dog, his son, the Lakers, and his new used car. I offered to pay my share of the pizza and he happily accepted. We then went for a walk on the Santa Monica Pier where I learned that Mike was still a photographer but now was taking pictures of children in a mall. He took my hand as we walked, but my heart felt nothing.

What had happened? Where did the chemistry go?

At the door, Mike gave me a little hug and wished me well. We both knew there would be no passionate kisses and no playful sex. Our time had come and gone.

> *Note:* What used to be is not always
> what your heart currently wants.
> I had grown. He hadn't.

False Teeth and Comb Over

"Maury"

Oh God, another date with a man named Maury.

He showed up in a red nylon jogging suit for our Starbucks coffee in Santa Monica. He had a major comb over. He constantly played with his loose false teeth and used his tongue to splash coffee around his mouth like mouthwash. Maybe he had a nervous condition. All I know is that he did horrible things with his tongue that were neither sexual nor socially acceptable. As soon as I said hello, Maury jumped into a narrative about his life. He had been divorced three times, he lived in a trailer near Redondo Beach, and he loved to play canasta.

> "It's not fancy, schmancy. But it's good soup and free. Free is good. What an adorable *punum* you have."

"Every Thursday night I go to the Jewish Community Center. They give us matzo ball soup before we play checkers. You wanna go with me this week?"

I just stared at Maury, not able to come up with an excuse. Maury continued in his Brooklyn accent.

"It's not fancy, schmancy. But it's good soup and free. Free is good. What an adorable *punum* you have."

His Jdate ad said he was sixty-one years old, retired, and financially comfortable. I say he was seventy-eight and living on Social Security. He looked so unhappy, so tired. He was poorly dressed, boring as hell, and didn't offer to pay for my latte. I felt sorry for Maury, but not sorry enough to share a matzo ball.

This date was fourteen minutes . . . three minutes longer than my date with Jumpsuit Jim and worlds away from what I was looking for in a man.

Note: When it's right, it's right.
When it's wrong, it's fourteen minutes.

On J-Date, I had found lots of single Jewish men. But the men consistently weren't what their profiles professed. On Match.com, I found love with Scott; on MillionaireMatch.com, I found liars. With the Matchmaking Mavens, I found a proposal; and at Starbucks, I found lust. So where would I find truth, companionship, and lasting love?

I vowed that my next date would be with someone substantial, someone my age or younger, and someone who would take me to a restaurant and happily buy me dinner.

Date Thirty-Three

Hating, Hostile, Bitter
"Bert"

I thought Bert would be all that and more.

His ad in the slick *Los Angeles Magazine* was on the last page and read as the winning date of the month.

Retired doctor, sixty, attractive, financially secure, searching for a woman who is emotionally and financially able to take care of herself. I'm looking for a companion. Not a wife. I love fine dining and fine women.

"A companion would be perfect—
a man who wanted to travel and
spend weekends with me without
the commitment."

A companion would be perfect—a man who wanted to travel and spend weekends with me without the commitment of laundry and cooking 'til the day I die. I liked what I read.

We talked. Bert was a neurologist and seemed not to like the idea of retirement. We met a few days later for dinner at a lovely steak house in Sherman Oaks.

On paper, Bert was perfect . . . good-looking, educated, and wealthy. But what I quickly learned was that Bert had no sense of humor and was down on life. Why was this man looking to date?

During the evening, I learned that Burt hated Canada. He hated Mexico. He hated all airlines because he didn't believe in nonrefundable tickets. He hated traveling because of the crowds and hated the steak he was eating and returned it to the waitress, three times.

Bert hated cell phones and hated commercial television. He thought our dinner rolls were doughy and the tomatoes were not ripe enough.

He hated children. It came as no surprise when he told me that neither of his children talked to him.

But there was something Bert did not hate. He was madly in love with the three racehorses he owned.

I wish the four of them a happy life together.

Note: What the paper says isn't always what the paper delivers.

The Architect
"Owen"

An architect should be creative and look at life with curiosity, creativity, and whim. I must admit, Owen looked whimsical. His head was bald, completely shaven, a task that he apparently worked on every second day. I sat there listening to the usual story of how his wife cheated him out of most of his assets and how she turned his children against him.

"You know, she took the house, the minivan, and even half of my 401k. The kids think I'm dirt because I left them."

"That's really too bad." I tried to understand but I really didn't.

"Well, I'll show her. I've created this idea of an inside out house. It's going to be huge. The whole industry is going to change because of me."

I listened to him tell me that all the other architects in the world were not as talented as he was. I listened to him tell me how life was not fair.

He looked like a bitter man and had a personality to match.

We had spent the requisite thirty minutes telling our stories when Owen abruptly got up, tossed his half-finished Starbucks coffee in the wastebasket, and said goodbye from halfway across the restaurant.

How rude.

How arrogant.

How relieved I was.

> *Note:* If you want bitter, get it
> from herbs, not dates.

The Fat Guy
"Harold"

Now, Harold was not physically fat. But, for years he had made his living collecting and recycling it from restaurants around Los Angeles. Harold was in the fat business.

We met on Matchmaker.com, and through our email correspondence and phone calls, I knew we would hit it off.

To be honest, I was scared out of my mind. I liked Harold. He had everything I wanted in a man. We had only been on three dates, but I already knew he was wonderful.

Date number one was lunch at my favorite restaurant in Chinatown. We talked about our families, how we hoped the remainder of our lives would play out, and the importance of laughter.

"I love playing practical jokes on people." Harold's smile showed off his perfect white teeth. "One time I put this undulating hand at the bottom of my refrigerator and scared my daughter to the point of peeing. Her, not me." Harold's eyes twinkled when he spoke of his kids.

"I know," I chimed in. "Laughter is a gift."

Within two hours, I received an email from my date saying what a wonderful time he'd had at lunch and how he wished it had lasted longer.

Second date was a visit to my house. We drank wine, chatted, and I initiated a long, soft kiss at the door.

Third date was movies, dinner, and a bit of making out on the couch. He wanted to move to the bedroom but I said we had to save something for another date.

When Harold left, I immediately got on the phone to Peg.

"Why am I pacing? Why am I so nervous? Why do I want it to be our thirtieth date and not our third?"

"Over mushu chicken on date number three with Harold, I visualized us getting married."

Peg got to the crux of the situation within seconds.

"What would it mean if this man really was 'the one'? It would change your life forever."

She asked if I was afraid of being hurt again.

I said absolutely. After all, my husband left me. Death is the definitive gone. And then Mr. Director could not commit and left.

Do I dare chance having strong feelings for a man again? I must want to find love. Otherwise, why would I be putting myself out there on all of these dates? Yes, I wanted to find *the one*. I wanted to find the man who would again finish my sentences and know what I was thinking without saying a word. Can that happen twice? I was uncertain if it could.

Question! Why do most women immediately jump from just a good date to images of becoming life mates? Over *mushu* chicken on date number three with

Harold, I visualized us getting married. It was a simple ceremony and reception at either the Beverly Hills Hotel or Il Cielo restaurant . . . depending on how many friends and relatives he wanted to invite.

I had never met any of his friends or family and all I really knew about this man was that he was tall, handsome, intelligent, successful, had lovely manners, dressed well, and that, after three dates, he had not burped or farted once in my presence. My mind was at least four months ahead of reality.

A week went by and Harold did not call or email. What went wrong? I thought everything was going swimmingly. All I can think of is that I wouldn't go into the bedroom with him and I stopped him from unbuttoning my blouse. I guess those things are expected on date number three these days. If that really was it, then screw you, Mr. Fat Guy. And that's exactly the point—I didn't.

Note: Make sure you and your
date are after the same thing. In this
case, I was after a relationship;
Harold was after sex.

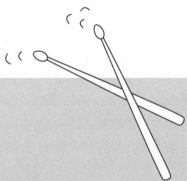

The Celebrity
"Bob"

I met Bob at Tower Records on Sunset. I was looking for a new reggae release and he was picking up an old Bob Marley.

"Hey, another person stuck in the Sixties."

"Are you talking to me?" I looked at the man standing two feet away.

"Sure. There's no one else around, is there?" He turned in a circle while twirling his hand above his head.

"I'm just stuck with the influence of the Sixties." I smiled.

I moved to the Top 40 section to buy the new Celine Dion CD. The man followed.

"Are you stalking me?" I asked in a friendly, almost flirting way.

"No. I'm Bob and I'd like to have coffee or dinner with you some time. Phone number?"

"I don't give that out to men I don't know." I paused and thought the situation through. "But you can give me yours, Bob. I'm Sherry."

I had been picked up in Tower Records. Amazing.

As I paid for the CD, I looked back to check the guy out.

Height: Five feet, eight inches.

Weight: A little paunch.

Hair: Shaggy brown, past his ears.

Clothing: Jeans and a T-shirt from Jamaica that read *No Problem*.

Age: Not sure, but probably around sixty. His face had lots of crags and lines, a sign that a lot of life had been lived.

Ethnicity: A Heinz mix of American, maybe a little British, with possibly a hint of African thrown in.

"Bob, why did you want to go out with me?" I asked a few days later when I called. I didn't think I was his type for a date.

"You just seemed nice. Look, if you don't want to go out with an old rocker, I understand."

"Old rocker?" Who was this man?

"Yeah, I used to play drums and sing backup with the . . . "

Since I had never been into rock music and had no clue about the group he'd just alluded to, I just faked it.

"No way. When did you guys break up?"

"Oh, back in '83. But we're planning a reunion tour. Agent is working on it as we speak."

Had I found myself a true rock 'n' roll bad boy? That seemed to be the current dating rage.

How should I dress to meet a guy who's had bras and panties thrown at him on stage? I wondered. I would have looked ridiculous in a short skirt. And my boobs were way too big for anything resembling a tube top. I had no stomach muscles to show midriff and my feet hadn't endured high heels in ten years. I decided on black slacks and a black sweater . . . safe.

We met at the House of Blues on Sunset Boulevard. Bob was seated in a booth in the VIP room when I arrived. With a nod, I knew this guy was someone I would like to get to know. Just looking at his craggy face made me smile. Maybe it was his squinty brown eyes. Or maybe it was just me fantasizing about how it would be to infiltrate the music scene. Dinners with Keith Richards and Madonna and backstage passes to party with Elton. I liked that dream.

"What are you writing? What kind of music do you like?" Bob seemed to be genuinely interested.

"I'm working on a murder mystery, set in Russia. And, I like all music except rap. And you?"

All the questions and answers were so banal. Bob

ate with impeccable manners and stood as I left for the ladies' room. The only sign of his ever having been a rocker was the tattoo on his left forearm. I couldn't make out what it was. His skin had wrinkled and the ink had faded.

"I'm teaching music now. But our tour is really going to happen. Sure of it." Bob was optimistic. I liked that.

We went to movies. We got hot dogs at Pink's, the famous stand in Hollywood. We even went to a chamber music concert at the Dorothy Chandler in downtown L.A.

I kissed Bob on our second date, and sadly felt nothing.

What makes a kiss or a touch magical with some men and not with others? It's unexplainable. All I know is it wasn't there for Bob or me.

Two weeks later, the call came.

"Hey, the tour is on." Bob was so excited. "We leave in three weeks for Vancouver."

"I'm real happy for you. Knock 'em dead." I didn't know the rock 'n' roll terminology for *break a leg*.

"Hope I can still keep up the pace. I may need something to help."

"Energy drinks?"

"No, sweetie. Snow. Old habits die hard and come back real easy."

That was the last time I heard from Bob. I'm sure he's having a ball on the revival circuit, playing every Indian casino in the country. This time around, he'll probably have bras the size of Michigan and Depends hitting the stage.

Note: Groupies come. Groupies go.
Sometimes just a glimpse into that
fantasy world is enough.

'Til Death Do Us Part
"Charlie"

Charlie emailed me from a profile I had on Millionaire-Match.com, the online site where no one was what the site's name professed. I really wasn't interested in going on another blind date. I was tired of being disappointed and was really confused and disillusioned by the whole process. Woman meets man. Woman or man doesn't like the other. Woman or man or both go away depressed.

But what the hell, I'd try again. It was only time and at that moment, I had more than I needed.

I emailed Charlie.

"Glad you liked what you read. Tell me more about yourself. Your profile was vague."

Invariably, a dating profile will answer the question, "What do you do for a living?" It's usually the first thing a potential date checks out. From this answer, you can sometimes glean an idea of what your date will be like. You know that if the man is a sales clerk, you won't be dining at Spago and he won't be pulling up in a Jag. Wait a minute. Maybe his ninety-year-old father owns the business and is insisting his son learn it from the ground up. I used to know this guy who managed an apartment building. Turned out that his father was one of L.A.'s largest real estate developers and sonny was learning how to fix toilets and rent space so when Dad went to the big unfurnished pad in the sky, he'd be ready to play with the big boys.

> *Note to self:* Never decline a date
> because of a profession.

Charlie had put nothing in the space for occupation.

He wrote back and said he used to be a stockbroker, but because of the bear market, he'd sought out and trained for a new livelihood. He didn't say what.

He had never been married and was fifty-five.

Red flag. Why hadn't this man been able to commit to a mate? Was he difficult to get along with? Was he commitment-phobic? He must have wanted to be in a relationship. Why else would he be on a dating website?

I decided to give Charlie a chance. Listen, after all the frogs I had kissed, it was a wonder my lips didn't have warts the size of oranges. Why not one more?

We met three days later at a California Pizza Kitchen for lunch. I ordered my favorite CPK salad and Charlie had a small pizza. He was nice. Average looking, a bit serious. He told stories about living in Peru and working as a sheepherder and how, when he finally got a chance to visit Machu Picchu, the altitude made him throw up the entire time he was there. He should have kept that information to himself, at least until after we ate.

It was an okay lunch. I wasn't wowed by Charlie but gave him my phone number figuring he was more interesting than the architect and better looking than Mr. Comb Over. I still didn't know what he did for a living but he must have had some job. He paid.

The following day, the sheepherder called and invited me out for Saturday night. I gave him my address.

"I thought we'd catch *Our Town* at the Victory in Burbank. How does that sound?" Charlie seemed enthusiastic about getting together and about his choice of entertainment.

I wanted to say it sounded like a date I had in eleventh grade but accepted Charlie's offer.

"Goodbye, Mama. Goodbye, Papa. Goodbye, Grovers Corner. Goodbye . . ."

It was the third act and Emily didn't want to be dead.

Charlie's cell phone vibrated. He went out to the lobby. Three minutes later he found his way back through the dark theater, leaned over, and whispered that he had to leave.

"Is there a problem?" I presumed there was.

"Yes, I have to go to work. Immediately. Do you want to stay?"

"Shhhhhh." The lady next to us was annoyed. Emily was still saying her goodbyes.

"No, I don't want to stay." I actually could have left the bad production after Act One.

"Well, then you have to come with me. No time to take you home. Hopefully, I won't be long."

I was going to see where Charlie worked. My curiosity peaked. What kind of job would need someone at ten in the evening? Maybe a plumber or a doctor? No, he would have told me if he were a doctor. Maybe Charlie was a police detective or an airport security chief. Or maybe he was a drug dealer who had to pick up a delivery from his Peruvian connection.

We drove only ten minutes and stopped in front of McMurray's Funeral Home.

"Why are we stopping?" I asked, hoping he had made a wrong turn.

Charlie leaned in close. "This is hard because women hate . . . okay, I'm a mortician. I embalm bodies and prepare them for burial. It's a recession-proof business." Charlie stared at me to see how much I was freaking out.

"I'll just wait for you in the car."

"It's not a great neighborhood. I can't let you do that. You have to come in."

I followed, hesitantly, through the back door of the mortuary. The place had a musty odor; in my mind, it was the smell of death.

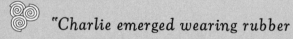
"Charlie emerged wearing rubber gloves, a clear mask, and a gown like you see in operating rooms."

"You can sit here in the hallway. I'll find out what's going on."

No wonder this man didn't want me to know what he did for a living. Sure, someone had to fill people with those preservatives, but I didn't want it to be the man I was dating.

Charlie emerged through swinging doors wearing rubber gloves, a clear mask, and a gown like you see in operating rooms.

"There's been a huge car accident and I have to work on three bodies."

"I have to get out of here, Charlie. I couldn't even go in a mortuary to choose a casket when my husband died."

The idea of death had haunted me for years. Where was my husband? Was there a heaven? I had even gone to a psychic who was supposed to be able to communicate with the dead. Apparently, my husband had laryngitis the day of my reading. Contact didn't happen but she still took my *donation* of one hundred dollars.

Suddenly, a loud noise jolted my senses as one of Charlie's associates crashed through the double doors pushing a gurney.

I screamed. There was a dead, bloody body right in front of me.

"Oh my God, I didn't know anyone was back here." The associate turned red with embarrassment.

I turned white and thought I would faint.

Meanwhile, Charlie was trying to calm us both down.

"Here, take my car." He handed me his keys. "I'll get a cab to your place when I'm finished. Bob, get that body out of here."

About four hours later, my security buzzer rang. I saw Charlie through my little television screen and announced that his keys were with the guard in the lobby.

I now realized why Charlie left "Occupation" blank.
Death is not an aphrodisiac.

> *Note:* Be up-front about what you do
> for a living, even if it's taking care of
> those who aren't.

Date Thirty-Eight

I'm a Young 89
"Saul"

It was time to move out of Los Angeles. I was tired of the noise, smog, and congestion. L.A. had been good to me. I'd worked. I'd learned. But something told me I needed another fresh start.

It was hard leaving my friends, but I knew we would stay in touch. Too bad it's never the same. You call, you email, but you're not down the hall or around the block.

I visited Las Vegas and the west coast of Florida and finally chose the beautiful desert of Southern California. Las Vegas seemed a bit too transient and Florida was too far from my children. I had a few friends in the Palm Desert area and I knew they would lessen the loneliness of moving into a new community.

Here, in the quiet, smogless, warm, dry climate of the desert, I intended to write a great novel, knit lots of sweaters for my grandsons, learn how to play golf, and retire gracefully.

The dating scene was behind me. I had not given up on love but had no desire to pursue it.

It took weeks to get my new home set up. Pictures were hung, electronics connected, furniture delivered, and landscaping finished. I liked it. It felt good despite the 105-degree weather outside. I could walk right from my great room into the pool, which stayed a cool 96 without the heater. It was July in the desert but I didn't care. I liked new beginnings.

Finally settled in, I went online and saw that I had eighty-seven emails. Most were spam, some were from friends, and one was from J-Date.

"You've got J-Date Mail."

I had forgotten I was even on the website. Months

earlier, I'd changed all of my online profiles to my desert location, alerting old dates that I was moving and sending out available signs to possible new suitors.

"I see you just moved to the desert. My name is Saul and I'm a songwriter. Please don't let my age scare you away. I'm a young eight-nine and have lots of energy. I hope we can have tea or coffee together and chat."

I checked out Saul's profile. Eighty-nine years old? *There is no way I'm going to go out with an octogenarian,* I thought.

"I didn't hear back from you. Please write. Your profile sounds so interesting and your face is adorable. I really am a nice man." Saul had emailed again.

I wanted to be polite, so I sent a note.

"Saul, thank you for contacting me, but I think our age difference is just too wide. I wish you the best in your dating search."

I was sure that would end the man's pursuit.

I was wrong. Saul wrote again with his phone number and several reasons why I should call.

"I've lived a fascinating life. Fought in the Big War and have stories to share. I still play the piano. I've won a Grammy . . . "

The most compelling and interesting reason was that he really wanted someone to talk to about music.

My first date in my new city and it was with someone who would probably look like a shar-pei.

Saul was seated at an outside table at The Fisherman, a casual local restaurant. I was right. He did look old and wrinkled with white bushy eyebrows and a rim of white hair around his head.

I sat down ready for a tedious lunch with boring conversation about yesteryear.

To my delight, I was totally wrong. This eighty-nine-year-old fellow had energy. He laughed and was so animated that I completely forgot about his age. Saul had written songs for Rosemary Clooney, The Andrew Sisters, and Johnnie Ray. He told me stories about how musicians traveled the country during the great depression, playing in bars for room and board.

"Once, I hitched a train from Baltimore to Miami with just my clarinet and a tux. I wanted to get to Cuba. That's where the action was. Great music was being written there."

"Did you make it?"

"Ah, yes. And I learned to rumba. I played at La Tropicana with amazing Afro-Cuban musicians. What a time." Saul's face lit up as he reminisced.

I sat there listening, wanting to be his daughter. His eyes sparkled when I asked questions. He was alone. He had outlived his wife and his son. He had no contact with his only grandchild back East and had lived in his desert condo for over twenty years.

"Saul, come over for dinner Thursday night. I'm not a great cook, but I can whip up something. I'll pick you up."

"No need. I'm still driving."

As we left the restaurant, Saul took my arm and patted it twice as if to say thank you.

I cooked a pot roast on Thursday. It was the first time I had used my new oven. The smells of the slowly simmering vegetables and meat engulfed the rooms and made my house feel like a home. I bought flowers for the table and had programmed my stereo to play a combination of Tony Bennett, George Shearing, and Frank Sinatra.

Seven o'clock came, and went. Saul didn't show up. I called his house, but no one answered. I worried.

Saul never showed up. I didn't know where he lived.

On Friday, I called his number at least six times and finally got an answer.

"Hello?" A woman answered the phone. "Who's calling?"

"I'm a friend of Saul's. Who is this?" I responded, very confused.

"A neighbor. Molly Lissman. Saul passed away yesterday. He had a heart attack around two in the afternoon."

"I see. I'm so sorry." I hung up the phone.

My eighty-nine-year-old date had died. I only met him once but I was sad. Saul had touched my heart.

Note: Love has no age boundaries.
We seek it until we die.

Stud Muffin Two Again
"Matt"

In all truthfulness, I really never did stop seeing Camera-man Matt, except when I was in love with Scott. While dating Charlie, Bob, Harold, Owen, and the others, Matt came drifting in and out of my life.

The phone would ring, he would be in town for a few weeks, and we would hang out. Still no flowers, no actual dates. Nothing had changed. We would go to dinner or a movie, and when I moved to the desert, we'd play slots at an Indian casino and have the all-you-can-eat buffet at the club. Sometimes he would pick up the check, sometimes I did, and sometimes we would go dutch. Sometimes we would have sex, and other times it was just a hug at the door. I seldom had Matt spend the night. I wasn't used to the sound of snoring or sharing my bed for eight hours.

Even though I didn't love Matt in a romantic sense, the comfort of having a good male friend was assuring. Did I want to be in love with Matt? Yes. But as we all know, love can't be forced.

What is the difference between love and chemistry? For me, the clue that I was in love with my husband and again with Scott was that I wanted to be with them every day and thought about them when I wasn't. If something wonderful happened in my life, they would have been the first to know. If I was sick, I wanted the person I loved by my side. If I was in a store, I thought of buying for them before myself. Their touch was comforting and being by their side made me feel proud.

The unexplainable force of chemistry is animalistic. Whatever vibes, inexplicable energy, smell, or feeling a person gives off just happens to mesh with your sensual makeup.

Matt's energy meshed with mine, but when he wasn't around, he wasn't in my mind or my heart.

> *Note:* How do you know if it's love or just chemistry? It's sometimes hard to distinguish the two but when true love happens, it will be both.

Singles Night Out with "The Geezers"

All my new neighbors were married and thought I should be too. They took an immediate interest in giving me suggestions on how to find a partner. According to Desert Dating 101, the best way to meet men was to join the Singles Night Out Gang. It wasn't an official gang. The cops weren't beating down doors looking for members. It was just the thousands of retired men and women of the Coachella Valley who frequented the bars and clubs scouting the opposite sex for dancing, companionship, and fun.

I wasn't interested in becoming a member.

"How about Friday night?" My single friend Renate was on the phone.

I didn't want to go. I had never been part of the singles bar scene. I didn't know how to troll.

"It's just one night. Let's try it. We've got to put ourselves out there." Renate won. I had a date Friday night with my beautiful, tall, thin, blonde, German friend. Would anyone look at me?

Our route would be the Sullivan's Steakhouse bar area, followed by The Nest, a notorious hangout for older singles.

Ready, bait, troll!

Sullivan's was so packed you couldn't see the floor. Loud music played. Nice, casual dress was taken to a higher level. The men were spiffed up in their après-golf sweaters and the women all had on high heels and chandelier earrings. As each new female entered the room, she was checked out by the tribe of old, hungry bachelors sitting at the bar.

And the race was on. Who would be the first to

approach the new competitors? *Argyle Blue was in the lead, followed by Cashmere Brown. On the outside, Purple Button-Down inched closer while Orange Bow Tie pulled up the rear. And the winner was . . .*

"Can I buy you ladies a drink?" Cashmere Brown inquired.

"We haven't had dinner yet. But thanks." Renate glared at me. I guess my answer was wrong.

"You always accept a drink. It's polite, even if you're not interested in the man. Then the others see you being approached by someone else and they come over. It's the game." I had a lot to learn.

Standing in the center of the packed room, I felt like a cow at auction. *Who will give me $200 for this great lady? She has a few miles on her and a little beef but still can be milked for all she's worth.*

Dinner was over and it was time to move on to The Nest. No luck or interest at Sullivan's.

The crowd at the new haunt was more eclectic. There were fewer sweaters and more men with hair in their ears. None was younger than sixty-five. In contrast, there were plenty of women in their forties, all probably looking to wrangle a rich, older man. Many

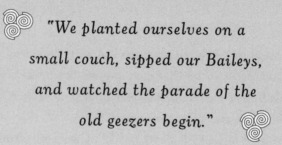

"We planted ourselves on a small couch, sipped our Baileys, and watched the parade of the old geezers begin."

seemed to be regulars. All were holding a drink and scoping the room.

We planted ourselves on a small couch, sipped our Baileys, and watched the parade of the old geezers begin.

It was like a conga line of men walking by to check out the goods. The bald, the bold, and the bountiful strutted their varied bodies by our table. Some winked, some asked if we wanted a drink, and others quickly moved on to younger pastures.

The beautiful and determined women placed themselves as close to the entry door as they could. They fought for this strategic position like soldiers in battle. The more unremarkable and shyer women took tables toward the back, hoping they would be noticed by a similarly challenged man trying to find some space in the overcrowded room.

There were the local cowboy geezers who just kept going from one woman to the next trying to win a dance.

There were the serious geezers: "What do you think about privatizing Social Security?"

There were the Southern geezers: "Ma'am, I would be honored if you would allow me to purchase you a gin fizz."

And there were the sleazy geezers, who just stared.

It was so dark that you could hardly see anyone's face. I'm sure that was intentional. Too bad I had wasted a half hour on my makeup. The bar and piano areas had Christmas-style white lights strung around for decoration and Tahitian fans hanging from the ceiling. A pianist played.

Picture the *Casablanca* bar on drugs and you can see The Nest.

The cruise ship dancers hit the floor for every song. They dipped and swirled and shimmied like pros. They were the people who learned their moves on Princess or Carnival. Onlookers applauded and hooted. The dancers who had not been either on a cruise or to Arthur Murray's stayed more to the sides and back.

Our waitress came over. "Can I get you something else to drink?"

We chimed together that we were fine.

"This is my first time here." I proudly told Waitress Mary this fact. "Do you know any of those men?" I pointed toward the lineup at the bar.

"Oh, those guys? They're regulars . . . four Jews with prostate problems." Renate and I cracked up. We couldn't stop laughing.

"You sound like you're having way too much fun." A nice-looking man, around seventy, approached and sat down on our sofa, squeezing Renate and me way too close. We settled into a conversation with John. Within three minutes, we learned that he had been widowed two years earlier, had lived in the desert for six years, had two children in Los Angeles, didn't have a steady woman in his life, and preferred women around his own age who were sophisticated, smart, and not money hungry. He told us just about everything but his Social Security number. I think he was eyeing me over Renate. Was he blind?

John moved away when the polite conversation became quiet. Within a minute, we saw him dancing with a woman no older than forty, dressed in tight jeans and a strapless top, with wild red hair. He was cupping her ass and smiling from ear to ear. So much for John's altruistic claims. That man was just after some booty.

Meanwhile, a tall, not very good-looking cowboy sauntered over and asked Renate to dance. She politely turned him down. For the next ten minutes, man after man after man came over to our table and asked my blonde friend for a whirl on the dance floor. It was a race to see who would win.

After six refusals of men who were far off her dating radar, we left and decided that we did not have the makeup to become members of the Singles Night Out Gang. I was home by 9:15 PM.

> *Note:* What's right for some is just
> too uncomfortable for others.

Epilogue
All the Rest

During the next year, my dating calendar was totally blank except for my once-a-month visits from Matt. Somehow, though, the interesting emails and phone calls continued.

Ring.

"Hi. This is Charlie. Remember me, your friendly mortician? You've changed your telephone number. Have you moved?"

Ring.

"Hi. This is Randy. I overheard you giving the sales clerk at Best Buy your phone number."

You've Got Mail.

"Saw your profile on Jdate.com. I live in Tel Aviv but want to come to the United States. Maybe we could strike up a friendship."

You've Got Mail.

"Saw your profile on Matchmaker.com. Noticed you are in the entertainment industry. I'm twenty-seven and would like to be an actor. Can you help me? If you do, I'll do something for you that will keep you smiling for days."

Ring.

"Hey, Babe. It's Lenny. Guess what? I bought a place down in the desert and thought we could pick up again. I know you love me. And, my dick works better than ever."

You've Got Mail.

I stared at my computer for at least ten minutes wondering if I should open the MillionaireMatch.com email. Finally, I pressed Delete and systematically went to all my dating sites. One by one, I said goodbye to my online dating partners. Delete. Delete. Delete. My profiles were history.

It's been ten years since my husband died. Funny, I thought I would be married and settled into a new relationship by year two. Instead, it's been nine years of dating, lusting, and looking for love.

And in the end, I'm still single.

There were many dates I didn't go into detail about: the accountant who whistled through his teeth when he talked; the dentist who presented me with a box of Sensodyne toothpaste on our first date; the actor who wore a very bad toupee; and the retired sea captain who wanted me to sail around the world with him on his forty-two-foot sloop. There was the veterinarian who contacted me once a year to see if I had found my true love, the young Latin who thought I should be honored to date him, and the man who divorced my friend and wanted to date me.

There was the agoraphobic author who could never get out of his house to visit me and the friend of a friend who just wanted an arm piece to cover up the fact that he was gay. There was the younger producer who I desperately wanted to date and the rabbi I didn't.

I could have married Lenny. I wanted to marry Scott. I had two wonderful relationships with younger men and have had many laughs along the way. In another year, I'll reach the deadline Stud Muffin Matt and I set up—our pact to move in together after five years so we don't grow old alone. That won't happen. I'm not old or bored enough yet to settle. Life is still just too damn much fun.

Ten years ago, I slept on my side of the bed with Dooley Dog on the other. Now, it's all mine and I use every inch. I thought I needed a man to make me whole. That's what many of us baby boomers were taught. That's rubbish. I'm complete by myself.

I now own a power drill and know how to varnish a door. I eat alone in any restaurant I choose and go to the cinema by myself. I travel the globe alone and can go to my house of worship and talk to God without self-pity or anger that I'm not with a partner.

I work. I create. I live.

Quite simply, I am once again the woman my husband fell in love with. And for that, I have to thank the Davids and Maurys and Bens and Matts. With each one of them, I learned something new that inched me along the way to a healthy single life. All the good dates gave me confidence. All the bad dates showed me what I didn't want in my life.

But being happy with the single me doesn't mean that I will stop dating. It means that I'm at last ready to date. I still believe Mr. Right Again is out there waiting to show up at my door with that red bow and a great big smile.

Do you remember that *Personal Perfect Man List* I put on my refrigerator? As soon as I finish this sentence, I'm going to tear it up. There is no such thing as a perfect man. We all have flaws, imperfections, and scars. We're human. It's all about compromise, chemistry, and timing.

When I least expect it, when I've used up every drawer in my bedroom dresser and every inch of my closet; when I've gained ten more pounds and see age spots sprouting on my hands, that's when my Not So Perfect Man will most likely appear.

Just in case you know someone who would like to meet a nice Jewish Nana who loves the water, loves dogs, can't cook, but is great at choosing restaurants, be sure to call me at 555-13 . . .

> *Note:* Never give up on love while
> loving the person you are.

Acknowledgments

I've lived this book for ten years . . . so there are many people to thank.

First, thank you to every man I have ever dated. If you think you are in the book, you probably are. I'm sure you didn't realize I was taking notes.

Thanks and love to my wonderful children . . . my son and daughter-in-law, Justin and Nga Trinh-Halperin, and grandsons, Milo and Khai Halperin. Your love is my most cherished gift and your support is my power. To my son Jonathan Halperin, I love you.

Special thanks to my editor, Brooke Warner, who took my dream and made it a reality. You are an amazing and talented woman.

To the entire Seal/Avalon team, thank you for your patience, creativeness, enthusiasm, and trust. I bow to my designer, Domini Dragoone; my managing editor, Marisa Solís; and my PR über-lady, Krista Rafanello.

My dear friends Melody Kielisch and Giorgio Aristo, thanks for bringing out my best creativity and telling me I can do anything.

A huge thank you to my wonderful friends mentioned in the book. You patiently lived through every date with me: Peg and Buzz Gitelson, Janet Edwards, June Chandler, Renate Stielhack, Bronwyn Miller, Nanci Linke-Ellis, and Erica Keeps.

Thanks to The Monday Night Writers: Margaret Seeley, Jack and Marci Stillerman, Joanne Hardy, Kathryn Jordan, Harf Windsor, and Les Rogers. You are all so talented and an inspiration.

To Jen Papineau, my super web designer, a huge thank you. You're amazing.

To Dr. Steve Galen, the best physician in the whole world, thanks for taking such good care of me. Hope I have another thirty years of you telling me to exercise more, eat less, and watch out for airport germs. Ellie, you're a dear.

And thanks to Judy and Jerry Halperin and Donna and Charles Paskin. You always have cheered me on, been there when I needed family, and supported my sometimes insane adventures.

Remarkably, I've stayed friends with many of my classmates from Beacon High School in Upstate New York. When I wrote and directed *The Senior Follies* more than forty years ago, you all told me that I had a future in show biz. So off I went. Thanks for believing in me all these years.

To Sarah Self, my agent with The Gersh Agency . . . Hollywood awaits. Thanks for believing.

And finally, I thank Warren. You've proven to be a hard act to follow.

About the Author

Sherry Halperin runs her own production company, SLH Productions, and has produced music concerts and ballets across the United States. Prior to that, Halperin had her hand in Hollywood for more than thirty years, where she worked as an agent, film distributor, and on many television shows as a writer, director, and producer. Halperin lives in Southern California with her pound-rescued dog, Bijoux. She has two adult sons, one daughter-in-law, and two young grandsons. Visit Halperin online at www.sherryhalperin.com.

Selected Titles from Seal Press

For more than twenty-five years, Seal Press has published groundbreaking books. By women. For women. Visit our website at www
.sealpress.com.

Above Us Only Sky by Marion Winik. $14.95, 1-58005-144-8. This witty and engaging book from an NPR commentator addresses facing midlife without getting hung up on the future or tangled up in the past.

The Unsavvy Traveler: Women's Comic Tales of Catastrophe edited by Rosemary Caperton, Anne Mathews, and Lucie Ocenas. $15.95, 1-58005-058-1. Twenty-five gut-wrenchingly funny true stories respond to the question: What happens when trips go wrong?

Reckless: The Outrageous Lives of Nine Kick-Ass Women by Gloria Mattioni. $14.95, 1-58005-148-0. This inspiring book documents the lives of nine women who took unconventional paths to achieve extraordinary results.

Italy, A Love Story: Women Write about the Italian Experience edited by Camille Cusumano. $15.95, 1-58005-143-X. Two-dozen women describe the country they love and why they fell under its spell.

Body Outlaws: Rewriting the Rules of Beauty and Body Image edited by Ophira Edut, foreword by Rebecca Walker. $15.95, 1-58005-108-1. Filled with honesty and humor, this groundbreaking anthology offers stories by women who have chosen to ignore, subvert, or redefine the dominant beauty standard in order to feel at home in their bodies.

I Wanna Be Sedated: 30 Writers on Parenting Teenagers edited by Faith Conlon and Gail Hudson. $15.95, 1-58005-127-8. With hilarious and heartfelt essays from writers such as Dave Barry and Barbara Kingsolver, this anthology will reassure any parent of a teenager that they are not alone.